TABLE OF CO

THE 3 STEP CURE TO BEATING INSOMNIA

Firstly let's get this straight. I am not a doctor, i'm not a psychologist, i'm not a sleep specialist. No. I am none of these things. What I am is a long term insomnia sufferer, at the time of writing this I'm still an insomnia sufferer. In fact as time goes by the only thing that's happening is it's becoming more severe. Which is why I'm writing this book. Many believe that the key to curing issues such as insomnia is to face them head on, which made me think I should give it a try. Maybe writing out my experience and findings will help me beat this horrible illness.

As I said, at the time of writing this I'm still an insomnia sufferer. At this point I have no idea whether this book will be called 'Curing Insomnia' or 'My Experience With Insomnia.' Even just talking about the subject that hurts me mentally, why is this happening to me? I understand that there are worst things in the world than insomnia and some may give there right arm to be in my position but it's effectively ruining my life.

Hopefully I can figure out finally how to beat this and in doing so, help many others do the same.

OVERVIEW

Firstly I want to reiterate that I am not a sleep specialist or medical professional of any kind. I have managed, though, through self-experimentation, in-depth research and the help of sleep specialists to completely cure my own chronic insomnia. The techniques used are not ones that I have invented, they're a combination of techniques used over years with proven track records and new techniques that are innovative and effective. I have taken lots on board from some of the best in their fields such as Matthew Walker (sleep specialist), Hugh Selsick (sleep specialist) and Andrew Huberman (neurobiologist). I recommend anyone with sleep issues, looking for specialist advice, to listen to these before anyone else. Unfortunately there's lots of people on the internet in the modern day claiming to be experts, these 3 are definitely experts. I'm extremely thankful to all 3 for their knowledge and they're key to my success in beating insomnia. I would also thank my many therapists and GP, as they've been extremely helpful throughout.

I just want to be extremely clear as to what you can expect from reading this book. Suffering from insomnia myself I can completely understand that you aren't here to waste time. You want the answers as quickly as possible, as each sleepless night twists the knife deeper. Quite simply, I will lay the outline of this book, what you can expect to find, at which stage of the book. Then you can dictate for yourself as to which chapter you wish to begin.

The first stage of the book is similar to an introduction. I will explain who I am, my own experience with insomnia and how it's effected my life so far. I will then continue to explain how you should determine the difference between good sleep and bad sleep (not as simple as you may realise). I also run through a sleep diary, what it is and how you should be using one as an effective tool against insomnia. If you're completely familiar with all of this and don't need me to explain any further, then by all means skip this section. I would then recommend going straight to the chapter titled 'Sleep Hygiene'.

From the sleep hygiene chapter and onwards I take you through the gradual steps to beat insomnia, similar to what a medical professional will take you through. The reason we take it gradual is that we want to fix your sleeping problems with as little effect on your life as possible. For example, if just taking a hot bath before bed cures you, there's no need to completely change how you live your life. Instead we want to try gradual steps, each one getting slightly more serious and will have a bigger impact in your usual way of living. This will cover things such as sleep hygiene, reading books, noises to help sleep, less blue light, breathing patterns and more. During this section I will run through exactly how I found each step, as these are the same steps I took with my insomnia. I will also include evidence and information about why each method should work. In some cases it will also include information as to why it may not work for you. These smaller steps can be very effective for people who suffer from milder forms of insomnia. They will also be effective for people that may not suffer from insomnia but are just looking to get better quality sleep. Unfortunately for chronic insomnia sufferers they won't be as useful. If you feel like you've covered all the small steps there is and you're still suffering with insomnia, please skip straight to the final '3 step cure for insomnia' chapter.

If the smaller steps do not work for you, then you'll need to make more significant changes to your lifestyle. The 3 step insomnia plan at the end of this book, is your best bet to putting your insomnia to bed (pardon the pun). Using only the most effective techniques and throwing the less-proven ones in the bin, this 3 step plan is exactly how I've gone from suffering with severe, chronic insomnia to an efficient sleeper.

Why should you use this plan instead of therapy? Well it's simple. I've read many different books, listened to podcasts and been to see many specialists. I've discovered lots of methods that are claimed to work in these mediums but have little effect. With research I found that there's little evidence to suggest they ever work, which does beg the question why do they suggest it? I also intend not to waste your time with this book. All my information is compact and truthful, unlike others, which are generally filled with 90% filler and 10% useful information. Moreover I intend to dumb down lots of the scientific jargon that specialists go through. Although extremely intelligent people, you often find yourself getting bamboozled by the way they word things, it's difficult to make sense of it all. In this book I will write simple and be straight to the point, making it less tedious to read. Finally and the 2 most important reasons for choosing this book, is time and money. Sleep therapy and sleep clinics with top specialists will always be leading the way in which insomnia is cured. However they take up time throughout your day, often having to take time off work to squeeze in sessions. Whereas you can read this book whenever you have time in your own schedule. This doesn't include the ridiculous wait times that can occur when waiting to get on a therapy course. Throughout the world each country will no doubt have different average lengths you will need to wait for therapy. In the UK lots of CBT therapists will have you waiting for over 1 year, which is just completely unacceptable and unfathomable. Whereas you could read this entire book in a matter of days. Then we have the financial burden. Again dependant on which country you live but therapy can be extremely expensive. Even if the therapy itself is free, it can still hit your wallet if you have to take time off work for sessions. Whereas this book will always remain a valuable price.

Quick Disclaimer: Although I have already reiterated my thoughts, I would just like to disclaim, there's no substitute for sleep therapy. I firmly believe this book can cure any chronic insomnia and the convenience of it being a book makes it ideal. However going to an actual sleep clinic or sleep specialist is always the most effective treatment, as it can be tailored to you.

WHY ME AND WHY YOU?

Who am I? My name is Ben Dye and I'm a man currently living in Newcastle Upon Tyne in the North East of England. I was born in a different part of England called Grimsby, on the 1st of February 1994. Growing up I loved playing sports, like any normal kid. I loved playing outside, like any normal kid and I loved getting into trouble, like most kids do. However unlike most normal kids I always had a problem with my sleep.

As far back as I can remember, maybe back until the age of 11 or 12, I can remember having issues with sleep. Firstly by the unfortunate circumstance of someone bringing a poltergeist book to school when I was a mere 8 years old. Yep, didn't sleep well after seeing that. Then, when I was around 10 years old watching the grudge at my mates sleepover, yep, didn't sleep well after that either. Unfortunately though these weren't the most sinister reasons for my lack of sleep.

Growing up my bouts of insomnia continued. However never seemingly altering my lifestyle or having a detrimental effect on my living. I gradually just began to live off less sleep than the average boy growing up. A skill that was something I would require later in life.

The first chronic insomnia I ever suffered was around the age of 16 years old. As a matter of fact it occurred directly over my 16th birthday. Which is typical as this was the first birthday I had ever gone all out. I was at the age where I was drinking with friends on weekends, partying Friday's and Saturday's, that's what 15 year old boys do in the north of England. For this birthday then I had it all planned out. My friend had a house we could go to, we had organised getting some older friends to go in the shop to get our alcohol and we had invited around 90% of our top 2 school years to come. Unfortunately though it wasn't to be, not for me anyway. Leading up to the weekend I had my first extreme dose of insomnia.

On the Monday I failed to sleep a wink. Meaning the next day I took time off school. Which shows how bad I must have been, due to the fact my mother would normally make me go to school even with a broken neck. This proceeded to effect me all week, even right through to the weekend. Throughout the week I had 3 days of 0 sleep and even on my other nights I barely made up for it. Meaning I missed my big party on the Saturday and I was heartbroken. All my friends went and still to this day talk about how that party was one for the ages. Gutted! For the first time in my life, my bad sleep had been so bad that it had a drastic effect on my lifestyle.

All is not what it seems though. At this point in my life I had began, like many, smoking marijuana. At the time it didn't even cross my mind. However now looking back, I have strong suspicions that this may have lead to the insomnia. Which may be why after a week or so I began smoking again and it magically disappeared. This would be the last of chronic insomnia for some time. I stopped smoking weed completely at the age of 17 and fortunately there was no adverse sleep complications this time.

Throughout my teen years and early 20's, I was a bad sleeper. By bad sleeper I put it down as I would say I managed 6-7 hours a night, I would wake up multiple times a night and I often had restless nights of 3 or 4 hours sleep. Like I said I was accustom to this and I had learnt how to get by on less sleep than most. Like many people I found it impossible to sleep on a moving vehicle, making long flights a nightmare. I would also find it extremely difficult to sleep after too much drinking on a weekend, which is also very common. None of these, though, took much effect on how I lived my life.

My insomnia somehow cropped up again 7 years later. At the age of 22 I had gone travelling, 2 years in

Australia, 8 months in New Zealand and 3 months around south east Asia. It wasn't actually the jet leg or the travelling that bought back the sleepless nights. They, in fact, came back during my most settled period of them 3 years.

I had an 8 month stay in the same area of Sydney. I worked the same job, did the same hours each day and my whole body was in an ideal routine. This batch of insomnia was much different than my younger years. It wasn't drug induced or down to any significant lifestyle change. In all honesty I have no clue where it came from. Out of my 8 months in this apartment, the insomnia lasted for 2-3 of them months. It came in a different form to the previous. Known in the sleep game as 'Maintenance Insomnia'. Basically put, this type of insomnia means you get to sleep but have trouble staying asleep.

Mine was occurring almost every other night. One night I would fall asleep for a couple of hours, then wake up and not be able to sleep again. The next night I would be so exhausted I would sleep wonderfully. The cycle continues. This, though, lasted for a couple of months. I didn't change anything to fix it and I didn't even really let it bother me too much. I just lived my life and naturally, the problem just seemed to fix itself. It was the next fight with insomnia that would rip through my existence and subsequently change my life forever.

As I'm sure everyone who's reading this will remember, the year of 2021 was a strange one for everyone. It was the year that COVID-19 swept the entire planet. During this year the United Kingdom was put into multiple lockdowns. In fact at the time of writing this, we are currently still in a new partial lockdown, however with the current vaccine program and cases falling quickly, hopefully this is the end. It was the year 2021 that hit me hard. I was placed on furlough for 5 months. For people who don't know, furlough was a scheme used in England in which you stay at home whilst receiving 80% of your normal pay, from the government. Sounds like a dream? Well, it was for the first 2 weeks but after it becomes depressing and worrying. Will I have a job to go back to? Will this virus wipe out the country?

Another thing that suffered during this period was my sleep. I began by telling myself I would keep getting up at 7am throughout lockdown, so I don't turn into a slouch. However this became 7:30, 8:00, 8:30 and eventually just getting up when I felt like it. This had a massive effect on my night time routine. I could no longer get to sleep until 1am at the earliest. My body was completely out of sync. After furlough getting back to work was tough. Although I craved the thought of some sort of routine, what coincided was something completely different. I knew that my abnormal sleeping would make getting back to a work routine difficult. However. Difficult is a gargantuan understatement.

As my insomnia made it's triumphant return, it came back this time with much more ferocity than the previous. This time it came back seemingly for good, seemingly to ruin my life. Firstly once back at work it started to creep in. In fact I still had no idea what was happening was classed as insomnia at the time. It began with maintenance insomnia, similarly to the insomnia I suffered whilst in Australia. I was going to bed at my usual early bed time for work, 10:00pm. I was falling asleep perfectly but then at the early hours of 2,3 or 4 in the morning I was waking up. Once awake at this time I would fall in and out of a sleepless state. This was occurring constantly, almost everyday and didn't seem like it was going away anytime soon. However, I could deal with this type of insomnia and in all honesty it had very little effect on my mood or my life at all.

It then elevated to new levels. My maintenance insomnia went from maintenance to chronic. (Chronic insomnia is the most extreme form of insomnia.). More subtly put, chronic insomnia is when shit hits the fan. To begin with, it started once I had some time off work. Coming back to work after some time away is never easy and mostly something you don't look forward to. This time was worse, the night before my first day back was a complete nightmare.

If I were to total up every second of sleep I got the night before I went back to work it would come to 0 hours 0 minutes and 0 seconds. I managed to go to work and through the power of coffee I made it through. Only to get back to bed early that night and sleep wonderfully for 9 hours. This didn't worry me. Not at all. I was out of routine and I was pretty sure by the end of the week I would be back into a well routined sleeping schedule. Unfortunately this was light years away from what actually happened.

It started off once a week. Once a week in which I would have major sleep deprivation. Anywhere ranging from 0-2 hours. I think I need to clear up exactly what was going on in my mind at this point. All I could think was that this was temporary, that eventually my routine would kick back into place. The gyms were closed so I was doing workouts at home but the day after a sleepless night I would be too tired and use that as a rest day, no big deal. If I managed to get a couple of hours if was a bonus, I knew I could get through the next day, as I had managed to with 0 sleep some days. It was frustrating and it was annoying but at this point it wasn't taking over my life. I just assumed that all of this would sort itself out eventually. However it got worse. It did start to affect my life, in a bad way.

I noticed that it was happening when I wanted a good nights sleep. If I had a long day at work coming up the next day or something lined up with friends, I would want to get plenty of sleep. Thus putting pressure on myself and end up not being able to sleep at all. This went on and on for around 3 months. 1 night a week I wouldn't sleep, the rest I would sleep reasonably well. This was more than likely due to catching up on my well needed shut eye but I can't be too sure. I gradually started to realise this wasn't going to sort itself. This was something that I had to begin taking action against. By this point I had began going in to work late after days I couldn't sleep, I had also began to let it take over me mentally. Before I could just tell myself 'don't worry it's 1 day, I can get through it and have a good nights sleep tonight' . Alternatively I would tell myself 'having one night without sleep won't kill me and loads of successful people live off barely any sleep'. I saw myself as mentally strong but by this point my mental resilience had broken. Instead I found myself thinking 'I can't live like this anymore' and 'all want from my life is to be able to sleep'.

Now was the point I decided to take action and also where this book begins. This was not a short process it's taken me months and months to go through an unbelievable amount of different methods. Some working a little bit, some not at all. I've tried everything.

I just want you to understand that you aren't alone and there's many many others suffering like you. Including me. I've laid in bed and angry in the early hours, frustrated I can't sleep a wink, knowing I have a big day ahead. I've frantically searched on Google at 4:00am looking for natural aids to fall asleep. Lost time off work, let it ruin my mood, friendships and take hold of my entire life. Buying books online that are helpless, listening to experts that tell me what I already know. I've done it all and it's awful but it can be fixed.

Here is my guide of what I tried, in the order I tried them, how they worked for me and why 'scientists' think they work. It's also similar steps to what any medical professional will run through with you, if you go to them with sleep problems. You'll notice as we go through what I try becomes more extreme, as I became more desperate. To begin with I wanted a simple solution but later realised to solve this I had to go much deeper. Which is unfortunately the case for lots of chronic insomnia sufferers. Although I had to take this problem to much deeper lengths than I ever intended, in the end it was 100% worth it. I now no longer take sleeping well for granted and fully understand I am in a better position than I was in the darkest times. My aim through this book is to help you get to were I am now and enjoy life without having to worry about sleep.

GOOD SLEEP / BAD SLEEP

Fact: People believe that we all need 7/8 hours of sleep a night to function correctly. This is completely incorrect. This is an average that has been pushed on to us for years. Millions of people will be there most productive on less than this and millions of others will need more.

We need to first understand what constitutes to good sleep and what constitutes as bad sleep. You're probably sat there thinking well getting 8 hours of sleep is good and getting 4 hours is bad. Not correct. Although I was also led to believe this for many years.

During my deep dive into insomnia, how sleep works and how to achieve optimal rest, I was pointed towards a 'sleep guru' known as Dr. Hugh Selsick. One of the few medical professionals who's actually taken to sleep, realised the importance of it and researched it to understand how it all works. He also runs his own sleep clinic in the UK and is highly thought of, helping cure a range of sleep illnesses. It was through him that I first heard about how we should define good sleep and bad sleep. As a rule most people believe that you need a minimum of 7 or 8 hours sleep a night, to function at your most optimal. We are also led to believe that anything less than this can be damaging to our health. Even talks of certain diseases being more common in people that sleep less. Well, sleep is key if you want to be happy and healthy but the numbers you see and some of the notions that are commonly thrown around are, in all honesty, misleading.

Good sleep should be determined on how we feel. If you feel reasonably well rested most of the time, then the sleep you're getting is good sleep for you. Whether this be 9 hours or 5 hours it's irrelevant. Bad sleep is when you don't fall into the above. If you don't feel well rested most of the time. If you're constantly tired or rarely feel well rested, you're having bad sleep. Again irrelevant of the amount of hours you sleep.

However if you have some days were you don't sleep great and are tired, that's normal. A few days here and there of bad sleep isn't going to hurt you and is completely normal. When our bad sleep becomes sleep deprivation and starts to affect us badly and continuously, something needs to be done about it. When bad sleep occurs it's also not necessarily that you aren't sleeping enough but you may be sleeping too much. Yes, it's a thing and it's been proven, sleeping too much can leave you as tired as sleeping too little. Moreover, having a day here and there of bad sleep deprivation isn't going to damage your health. Yes it's more than likely going to effect you the following day but all in all you'll be fine. Don't worry.

If you wanted to check online for yourself you'll see experiments claiming sleeping too little can shorten lifespan. If you look again you'll find that experiments say sleeping too much can shorten your lifespan. Remember we're all different and need different hours. Some of the most successful people in the world openly say they sleep 4 hours a night. Whilst you can find others, just as successful, that may sleep 9+.

SLEEP DIARY

This is the last and final thing that I would like to point out before I delve into sleep helping techniques. A sleep diary is something that kept cropping up over and over again as I looked up solutions to my insomnia. It's a tool that pretty much everyone agrees is useful for insomnia sufferers. All you need to do is jot down roughly how many hours you think you're sleeping each night. I would recommend not to use a fit bit, smart watch or any other devise etc. These are generally inaccurate when it comes to measuring your sleep. (Another tip from Dr. Hugh Selsick.). Just make your own judgment about how much sleep you think you managed and write it down everyday. Some days you'll be surprised how energetic you feel when you don't get much sleep. This is due to having high-quality sleep.

High-quality sleep is much more beneficial than disrupted sleep and it's hard to differentiate the two. Many will feel that they've been asleep for 7 straight hours but in actual fact they could've woken up multiple times through the night, without remembering. Again it just comes down to how well-rested you feel as a guide to the quality of sleep you're getting.

For the sleep diary though you don't need to take any notice of what sleep you're getting, just how long you're having. Jotting down how much sleep you get gives you a better insight and an easier overlook on how damaged your sleep pattern has become.

SLEEP HYGIENE

Fact: According to the sleep foundation around 30-48% of older adults will suffer with some type of insomnia.

After months of sleepless nights my insomnia became worse. It started happening more and more. Some weeks I had 3 or 4 almost sleepless nights and my whole life slowly began to suffer. Still it was relatively new and I was optimistic that it would eventually self-eradicate. However I started to understand that I could help myself by changing up some simple habits and lifestyle changes. This was my first step and at this point I hadn't started writing. At this stage my insomnia had become somewhat of an annoyance but not a disturbance to my life. It was enough of an annoyance, though, that I had decided to take action. No longer could I wait around for it to fix itself and instead needed to intervene. This is also the original step that most doctors will tell you to try first, as it's very basic and could be a simple cure.

This first step then was the most mild and I did what most people do when they have an issue but don't want see a doctor. I took advice from my mother. Her advice was something that most of us have probably heard of before. That was to have a nice hot bath at night, to relax yourself, before going to bed. Something that I later realised is common practice and recommended by many, it actually goes by the term of 'sleep hygiene'. Meaning that people recommend a nice warm bath, some clean clothes to wear to bed (pyjamas, underwear etc) and brush your teeth, before you go to bed. It's believed that the combination of these processes leave you feeling relaxed, clean and ready for bed. Not only this but experts say that after a nice, hot bath your core temperature actually lowers. Which seems strange but apparently you become so hot during the soaking that after you get out, your body dumps all the heat out of your body. If true this could be another way in which a bath helps you sleep, as most people will vouch for, it's much easier to sleep when you feel cooler. Apart from this, though, the evidence of sleep hygiene helping you fall asleep is limited. Experts that push for sleep hygiene mainly say that it's the routine you form that helps you sleep. Taking a bath, brushing your teeth, putting on your PJ's, is all part of a process telling the brain it's ready to sleep. Well, this is what they claim. For me it was something that was ingrained into me from a young age, I've always brushed my teeth directly before bed, had a shower at night and put on a fresh pair of underwear. All I had to do then was swap out my shower for a hot bath and my insomnia should ease?

That's what I did anyway I swapped my shower for a bath every night to try and relax me before going to bed. The bath is a great relaxation tool and I could almost feel myself falling too sleep after a 10 minute soak. However it did nothing for my insomnia. As soon as I was out the bath, the relaxation quickly wore off and I found myself in a mental battle to sleep again. For me the sleep hygiene did pretty much nothing. Not even pretty much, it just did nothing. I trialled it for 2 weeks in total and looking back on my sleep diary over them 14 nights, I had 3 nights of 0 hours sleep and 1 night of 3 hours. Hardly successful.

This was, however, the first step I had taken to try and help with my insomnia and it was the most basic of steps. I never had much faith in just a nice warm bath being the cure for a chronic, mental disorder but worth a try. By this stage though as I was becoming more aware about my sleep deprivation and thinking about it more and more, the insomnia worsened. Now every night getting in to bed I was beginning to worry If I would sleep at all I, so I knew I had to move on to the next stage and try something different.

Moreover I actually became aware, a fair few weeks later, that sleep hygiene has been proven not to work for chronic insomnia. Again this was information that I heard listening to a podcast with Dr. Hugh Selsick. For the average person that has relatively normal sleep cycle patterns, a hot bath before bed can help them relax and may even help them sleep better. For people that suffer from chronic insomnia though, it has little chance of being effective. However. Although lots of experts and studies have now debunked the sleep hygiene myth, I still see some top-level experts recommending a hot bath for insomniacs. Which is why I suggest you to start here, try it for 2 weeks and who knows you could be the lucky person this works for. Job done. If you start to take a hot bath before bed and after a week or so you know it won't work, by all means move on from this step quickly.

Conclusion: Sleep hygiene is not a cure for insomnia (most of the time) and for me it did nothing whatsoever. I would still not deter people from trying it as we're all different and maybe if your insomnia is very mild, it could help eradicate the problem. Please not it's mainly an effective method for normal sleepers just to improve their sleep.

EXERCISE

Fact: Around 35% of adults sleep less than 7 hours per night on average. 60% of these say they don't feel any type of sleep deprivation.

Something that stuck with me for many years, was from insomnia days in Australia. I remember explaining to my boss, at the time, about the sleep issues I was having. He then told me some very simple advice that would continue to stick with me for years. He said 'If you can't sleep you haven't tired yourself out enough, try doing more exercise during the day, if you do enough you'll always manage to sleep well'. Well I wasn't sure if this was a hint to try get me to do more work or if it was something that actually made some sense. Therefore I decided to put it to the test. I had always been a person who worked out 4/5 days a week but in all honesty lifting weights never felt like it took much out of me. I decided to start running on top of my weightlifting regime. All behold I actually felt like it started to work. However, it's impossible to give a definitive answer as I wasn't struggling too much with my sleep at this stage.

This is a completely different test, though. This time I wanted to see if simply adding more exercise into my daily routine would help the sleepless nights. I was already exercising about 1 hour a day, most days of the week, so upping my exercise would be difficult. Not impossible though, I wanted to up my cardio output and instead of just 1 hour a day I went for 90 - 120 minutes a day.

In fact studies have shown that physical exercise and sleep have a bidirectional relationship. Which basically means that they help each other, going both ways. More exercise will help get better sleep, while getting better sleep helps you exercise better. In fact in the 2013 'Sleep in America poll', they found that for people who regularly exercise, 76-83% of them have high quality sleep. For peopler that don't regularly exercise this number drops to 56%. Not only this but exercise also has a highly positive effect on our mental health. When we exercise our body releases chemicals called endorphins. Endorphins are powerful chemicals that benefit our mental well-being. Endorphins are very effective at reducing stress and depression. In fact exercise is said to be an effective underused method of treating mild to moderate depression. Stress, anxiety and depression can be direct causes of chronic insomnia. Hence the positive relationship between exercise and sleep. However, although exercise can be a useful tool for beating insomnia, it can also cause issues with sleep. When we workout our heart rate is raised, our body temperature goes up and our adrenaline levels increase. All 3 of these can lead to issues in first drifting off to sleep. This is why it's recommended you don't take part in vigorous exercise within 3 hours of bed time.

Exercise is another common method that is touted by sleep professionals. Just the same as my ex boss believed, exercise has the ability to tire you out mentally and physically. This in turn should help you catch some shut eye. For me then, I decided to try increasing my exercise for a minimum of 2 weeks. In fact due to gyms reopening after COVID, my exercise regime intensified permanently. Unfortunately, though, it didn't help with my insomnia. Again, it didn't help one bit. Again, I didn't have very high hopes for this. In fact part of me believes that exercising too much almost made it worse for me.

I found myself laid in bed, for hours again, from my usual bed time of 10pm until 7am when my alarm sounded, without getting any sleep. However, to rub salt into the wound even more, this time my body was dead. I felt like my body sank into the bed, my arms were jelly, my legs felt like concrete but still my mind was on overdrive. Critically, when going to work the following days not only was I sleep deprived but my whole body was exhausted. This made the 9 hour work slog feel like I was participating in hell week for the navy seals.

I never had very high hopes that increasing my exercise would cure my insomnia. I knew that it would tire me out and feeling more drained but insomnia is much more of a mental issue than physical. It wasn't my body that I would have to beat but my mind, which is a heck of a lot more difficult. When telling people about the issue they just didn't get it. People genuinely looked at me with disbelief, accuse me of exaggerating or making out like I must be falling asleep without realising.

This was a significant stage for me as during this stage of the process, it began to impact my work life. Up until now I had managed to go into work everyday and plod along until the day was done, without too much hassle. However, it had gotten on top of me far too much and I began turning in to work late, far too often.

As I lay in bed, feeling my heart race, body temperature rising and my mind working on over drive. During this time I would try to refrain from looking at the time but I had to, otherwise I would be wondering what the time was, which would occupy my mind even more! Gradually I see the time go down. 1am 'so if I get to sleep now il have 6 hours sleep'. Check again it's 2:45am, 'still if I get to sleep now il get 4 hours which I can handle'. 4:00am, 'Please, please get to sleep now and I can manage on 3 hours. 5:30am, by this point I'm stressed, I'm angry and overly emotional so I say to myself 'Forget work, I'll text my boss telling him I'll be late and I'm going to lay here until I get a few hours sleep'. I would then text my boss and lay there, checked my phone again at 7:00am, roughly usual get up time, still no sleep. Lay there and lay there until I realise I now can't sleep due to the stress factor I'm missing work. I roll out of bed, head to work 2 hours late, still with no sleep and have a dreadful day to endure.

Fortunately for me my workplace were very understanding. I have never been the type of person to take time off work and they knew I only would for significant purposes. Well, this and the fact that they could see in my face I was completely zombified, they knew it looked bad. By this point I was also being urged by many of my friends to head to a doctor but I wanted to keep going and solve it myself. The way I've been bought up, a doctor should be used as a last resort and I was convinced I could still beat this thing on my own. I was also very worried about getting put on sleeping pills, which was the very last thing I wanted.

Exercise doesn't work for most insomnia. It can be a sleep aid and help people who suffer with more mild sleep issues but isn't the cure for most insomnia. However if you don't exercise whatsoever, maybe you're just not tiring yourself out enough and some exercise will, at a minimum, boost your chances of getting high quality sleep.

READING BEFORE BED

Fact: Some of the most successful people in the world openly say they live of 4-6 hours a night. Elon Musk, Barack Obama, Boris Johnson and Richard Branson have all been public in there lack of sleep but still extremely successful in their given careers.

This was the next step that I could conjure up before looking deeper into it. I'd started to do my research online, during the nights I couldn't sleep (how stupid). Reading up on certain methods and patterns that may help you sleep at 4am, whilst trying to sleep, is not advisable and very counter intuitive . I would then have no energy to do any research the following day but the next night I would be so exhausted I would sleep a solid 7 or 8 hours. Thus, forgetting the pain I had suffered 2 nights before and feeling that maybe my insomnia didn't need too much looking in to.

Luckily, I had a plan. I mentioned that I've always been a bad sleeper, my whole life, this included never being able to sleep on moving vehicles. Planes, buses, cars, boats, you name it! If it moved, sleep was impossible. Until I went travelling in my early 20's that was. I finally discovered a simple new tactic that allowed me to catch some Z's whilst travelling on long flights and long bus journeys. It would still be very little sleep and we're talking a matter of a couple hours during a 10 hour bus or plane ride. Unfortunately nothing compared to some of my friends, who had me green with envy. Watching them drift off soon after take off and falling into a comatose state, until we landed, was somewhat something to admire. However, though, it was still some sleep and just having a couple of hours is worth the price of gold compared to having no sleep at all. How did I manage this? I just read a book. Simple as that.

It actually started all to my friend Iain who til this day has no clue he helped so much. Travelling on a a several hour flight from Australia to Bali, as backpackers do, we had decided to go economy class for the cheapest seats, on the cheapest airline we could find. Regrettably for this long-haul flight it meant we had no TV and essentially no personal space. To begin with we played cards to pass the time, which we got bored of after around 20 minutes. Not helped by the fact we were so close we could practically see each others cards. After our enthralling game of cards my friend turned his attention to a book, whilst I turned my attention to playing games on my phone. Which again lasted 20 minutes until I was hit with serious boredom. Then my friend turned to me and asked if I wanted something to read, as he had multiple books in his bag ranging from fiction to non-fiction. Reluctantly I decided this could be the best thing to occupy myself, although I hadn't read a book myself since my school English lessons, I decided to give it a go.

The book was made up of 3 mini stories and in total came to about 400 pages. The first story told the tale of a police detective working on tracking down a notorious serial killer, something I found to be a good read. As I read on and read on, all of a sudden I was punched in the arm by my nonchalant friend. I had fallen asleep! Without any realisation or warning I had drifted off around 10 pages into the book, only to be rudely awoken as the food trolley cart had made it's way to us. Although quite furious at the fact he woke me up, when for the first time in my life I had got to sleep on a plane, I was more than happy to eat. Next begged the question, could I fall back to sleep? Well, I ate my food, I chatted briefly to my friends and debated what we would do on arrival Bali. Then I went back to reading my book. This time with the intention that it could once again send me off. Incredibly as I read through I could feel myself gradually get more tired as the book went on. After around 7 or 8 pages I closed the book and tilted my head, viola, once again I fell asleep! At the time I felt *like what a caveman must have felt like upon discovering fire. After this I continued to take books wherever I travelled. It never stopped helping me sleep and although I never was the perfect travelling sleeper, it was a vast improvement.*

Back to the present day and I had once again come back to the books for help. Ever since my travelling days ended somewhat 3 years ago, I hadn't touched a book. Luckily for me I lived with 2 flat mates who did read and had very similar interests as me, so I took a look at what reading material they had to offer. Finally I settled on my book of choice.. A real life story about the great Diego Maradona, one of the best football players ever to live, as well as a drug fuelled party animal. This book seemed right up my street. The plan would go as follows. Still head to my normal bed time of 10pm, already teeth brushed and ready for sleep. Then lay in bed and read my book, using the bedside lamp for light, until I feel myself dozing off, put the book on my bedside table and catch some shuteye. Believe it or not, it worked. Just as I remembered it did. I would maybe manage to get through around 10-12 pages, before feeling myself naturally drift off. The most impressive part for me was how it completely cleared my mind. Insomnia is very much mind over matter and for me this was especially the case, as I would often find as soon as the thought of not sleeping popped into my head, a restless night of mind games would ensue. Once reading though, this all seemed to change. I would become gradually more intrigued in the book and life of Maradona, until everything else in my mind had disappeared. Even once closing the book these thoughts would continue and quickly I would nod off.

Fact: According to a study conducted in 2009 by the University of Sussex, reading a book before bed can help with insomnia. The study showed that six minutes of reading reduces stress by 68%, clearing the mind and preparing the body for sleep. Dr. David Lewis, a psychologist and author of the study, says a book is "more than merely a distraction, but an active engaging of the imagination," one that "causes you to enter an altered state of consciousness."

Reading is simply effective at helping you wind down and feel calm. It's something that's used by millions of people worldwide as a way to shut off the outside world and ease anxiety or stress. It's also believed that people who read books tend to have higher-quality sleep, although evidence of this is limited. In fact overall evidence of reading a book to ease insomnia is also very limited, with some studies seeing a direct correlation but others showing nothing.

For me though reading helped massively and in all honesty completely cured me of insomnia, I even went around telling people I was fine and that dreadful episode of my life had ended. Unfortunately, once again, it didn't last. To be exact it lasted for 13 nights, just shy of 2 weeks. Each night getting 6-7 hours of sleep which is my optimal sleep zone. The night it messed up was a Sunday. Being unable to sleep on a Sunday is relatively common for lots of people, who have weekends off work but for me it was much worse. I managed a total of 1 hour asleep. Yes that means I went to bed at 10pm and managed to dose off some time between 5:30 and 6:00am. Completely sleep deprived. However I figured it may be a minor blip and carried on with reading before bed. It wasn't a minor blip but instead a major setback. 3 days laters the same problem occurred leaving me again, sleep deprived.

My mind had beaten me. I was finding it much harder to engage with my book and forcing myself to get through 10 or so pages. As soon as the book was closed, boom! My mind began to race. I forgot all about whatever I had just read and instead worried about how much sleep I would manage. However I do still, for some reason, have faith have that reading could help some insomnia sufferers. I, myself unfortunately don't possess the mind to be able to completely switch to a book, consistently. For me I need a certain book, certain conditions and certain mind-frame to allow me to get lost in a book. Others (luckier) people have the ability to become embedded in a book without much effort at all. Hence why I suggest everyone to try reading if they have sleep issues.

Reading is a great way to ease your mind and stop yourself overthinking before bed. It may help people sleep with less severe cases but as for chronic insomnia, unfortunately it may not be as effective.

SLEEPING AIDS

Fact: Around 10-30% of adults around the world will suffer with chronic insomnia at any one time. This is roughly between 700 million and 2.1 billion people!

For me, this seemed like the next feasible step. Although the reading had worked for a couple of weeks and then stopped, I decided to stop the reading before bed. In my eyes I thought maybe I would start relating the reading with struggling to sleep and continuing reading before bed could worsen my insomnia. Therefore, at this stage I ditched the books.

The next stage was something that seemed so simple but also one that I had put off for some time. It was to help myself sleep via sleeping tablets. However as these are basic, over-the-counter tablets they're classified more as a sleeping aid. Sleeping aids are a strange step to take. Some doctors will recommend them to you, whilst others may tell you to stay away. As they're generally mild and non habit forming, they should be safe to take. This will obviously depend on which ones you take, what country you live and many other factors. With me I went for mild sleeping aids and I recommend that you do the same at this stage.

I highly recommend against any strong sleeping pills or prescriptions as they're habit forming and can be like a life sentence.

For me though, I really wanted to avoid all tablets if possible. I understood the dangers which tablets can bring, such as becoming dependant on them to sleep and becoming addicted. However I was getting more and more desperate. I started to feel like I was losing out on a minimum of 2 days per week, which equates to 30% of the week, I was losing 30% of my life. I say this because the days after no sleep I was incapable of anything productive. I could just about manage a day at work, get home and do nothing. Couldn't go to the gym, couldn't go shopping, couldn't hold a conversation with someone, couldn't even cook food. Them 24 hours were a living nightmare.

I took the next step then, sleeping aids. As mentioned previously some doctors may recommend these and some will go against. I feel that as they're mild drugs, with little chance of habit forming, they're certainly worth a go. I only recommend that you take these on nights you're struggling to sleep and not just every night for the sake of it. Ideally don't take them more than one 1 night in a row and break it up, every other night as a minimum. I mean although some doctors recommend against them, surely if you can get away with just taking a pill 2/3 nights a week to cure your insomnia, it's worth a shot? I certainly believe so but understandably if you're too anxious about taking sleeping aids, feel free to move past this chapter.

For anyone who doesn't know, pretty much every sleeping aid in the UK will be branded differently but the chemical itself will be exactly the same. It's a commonly used chemical called 'diphenhydramine hydrochloride'. **Diphenhydramine is an antihistamine medicine that relieves the symptoms of allergies. It's known as a drowsy (sedating) antihistamine and is more likely to make you feel sleepy than other antihistamines.** For me the brand I went with were 'Nytol'. However as I mentioned, most over-the-counter tablets will contain the same chemical. In other countries I'm not 100% certain of the over-counter drugs available. However I would recommend looking for 25mg tables of diphenhydramine hydrochloride (although they'll be branded differently). My plan was to simply take the Nytol tables once I realised that I may be having a difficult time sleeping. In my eyes, as I normally would only have 2 or so days with no sleep, per week, if I just took the pills twice a week I would not become dependant on them. The other factor I had to be aware of was drowsiness. It was difficult for me to know if I would sleep or not and I wasn't too sure how long I should give myself to get to sleep, before popping a pill. I decided to see how I felt at the time and roughly give myself an hour or so to get to sleep, before reverting to the pills.

Fast forward then to my first time of pill popping. My normal bed time was around 10pm, at this stag and my get up was 6:50am. My intentions for this was that it takes me a while to get to sleep in general and then I would still have time to get roughly 8 hours of kip. Essentially if I'm in bed from 10pm even if it takes me an hour to nod off il still get around 8 hours sleep. My first night of taking Nytol I had waited until 12:30am before I decided it was time to take action. I didn't want to risk having yet another zombified day at work. I take the pill at 12:30am, I close my eyes, it's 6:50am and my alarm is going off! Just like that, it felt like the pill had somehow landed on a switch in my brain, that instantly sent me to sleep. In all honesty, without sounding too much like a commercial, Nytol worked incredibly well and would recommend. In fact I had technically only taken half the correct dosage. They have 50mg and 25mg options, I was taking the 25mg tablets, meaning theoretically I should be taking 2. Well I have the option to take 2 but why should I when 1 worked so well?

Fast forward again to 3 days later when I next had trouble getting myself to sleep. Slightly different story. This time I again went to bed at 10pm and again ended up taking a pill at around just after midnight.

This time, though, I found myself still restless, with no sign of feeling drowsy at around 2:30am, so, I took another pill. Boom. I was out cold. The only issue, that I took my second pill around 4 hours before my alarm and I woke up extremely groggy. In fact I felt groggy throughout the entire morning but and it's a big 'but', I did get some sleep. Which in my eyes is a win. Fast forward again 4 days later. Same process, same result. This time I didn't bat an eyelid going for the 2 pills from the off. As soon as the clock hit 12 and I knew I couldn't sleep, 2 tablets down and 5 minutes later I'm in dreamland. Fast forward again 2 days later this time. Same process, different result. The exact same process, again. Again, I couldn't sleep, again I took 2 pills at roughly 12 o'clock, this time I couldn't sleep. What do I do now? Ride it out and hopefully sleep? Take another pill or will that be too much? Well, at 3am, less than 4 hours until get up, I decided to pop my 3rd pill of the evening, which luckily worked. However this left me feeling like the walking dead again the next day but even worse I was frustrated and angry, another method that showed promise, seemingly gone. It was something I wanted to stick with though and I decided to keep my trial ongoing for a few more weeks but to no avail. Once again as had happened in every previous step, my mind had beaten me. I was now fully aware that these weren't strong enough for my condition and every time I took the pills, my mind was already convinced that they would not work. I even tried mixing up different brands, containing slightly different chemicals but 0 worked and I was back to square 1.

There we have it then sleeping aids showed some promise in my experiment but unfortunately the effects didn't last. This could have been due to my body becoming used to them and thus the effects becoming lessened. On the other hand it could just be another mental block as my mind was subconscious and aware this is not a full-proof method and therefore I would have sleepless nights. It's also fair to repeat that these are very mild tablets, the chemical itself is actually used to treat different illnesses and not just insomnia. However there's seemingly high amounts of reviews claiming sleeping aids have completely cured some insomnia sufferers. Hence why I believe it's definitely worth attempting, even just for a fortnight, as it could be a simple and effective method

Conclusion: Sleeping aids are very mild and generally aren't going to fix someone with severe insomnia. However, they can definitely make you drowsy and ease you into sleep, which may be a very simple cure to your sleepless nights.

NOISE

Fact: Almost half of all Americans say they feel sleepy during day more than 3 days per week. Meaning almost half Americans are getting bad sleep.

Next up to try was noise. Maybe seems like a bit of a stupid suggestion that noise could be the key to helping me sleep, when for most it keeps them awake. I am no exception. Some of my friends need there rooms totally blacked out without a spec of light to be able to sleep. However, for me growing up, I was the same with noise. For me I could happily sleep with the light on, no problem but I needed it to be as quiet as possible, being such a light sleeper, any sort of noise could wake me up. In fact this was reiterated to other sleeping problems I had just a couple of year previous.

A couple of years ago something occurred to me in my new bedroom. I only had one window and it was a sunlight on the ceiling. Which looks lovely and is a great touch on a nice morning, to have some natural daylight seep in. The only issue I had with my sunlight is when it rained outside. For anyone who has ever been in a greenhouse or conservatory when it rains, they'll understand how much it emphasises the noise of the rain. Well this was the same as my sunlight,

I began being woken up during the night with heavy rain, then being kept awake whilst the rain persisted. To battle this issue I decided to download an app called calm. An app that supposedly helps you calm down and can be used to help you sleep. I downloaded the app in the middle of the night, started my free trial and we were set to go. Next up I realise it helps you sleep by playing 'soothing' sounds that in general are supposed to help. Lord behold the first sound that is played…. Rain Falling. You couldn't make it up. Although sleep deprived and annoyed at the app, I still managed to chuckle to myself, what are the odds? Either way the app didn't work and there were no types of noise that helped me sleep, they actually made it worse. Eventually I found some comfortable, well-working ear plugs that I could sleep in and these did the trick on the noise front.. for now.

I do hate to diss on certain apps that genuinely are trying to help you sleep. I am fully aware that lots of people would actually find rain falling a soothing, sedative noise. In fact noise is one of the most common methods used worldwide helping people sleep better. Calm noises played through apps such as waves craving or wind blowing are very popular. Moreover the noise of a fan whirring through the night seems to be incredibly popular at blocking out sudden noises that may awaken you. All in all it comes down to white noise and pink noise at being the most effective for better sleep. White noise is what I've just mentioned it can be something like a fan constantly whirring or an air conditioning unit humming. It's a consistent low level noise that will ideally block out sudden loud noises that may disturb your sleep. White noise is extremely common for sleep problems and said to be highly effective. Whereas pink noise, on the other hand, is similar to the other sounds that I have mentioned. It can be stuff like the waves breaking or any noise that is deemed calming/soothing. Pink noise is often the favoured sound that is recommend for people with insomnia. Not only will it help drown out other loud, disturbing noises, it can help your mind wander to a different place and help relieve sleep anxiety. Hence why sleep apps will often focus on pink noise sounds played at night.

Now moving on to my own experience in what I found with noise and the relation it has with insomnia. Well one thing I failed to mention was my ability to sleep when watching TV. I have no idea why but for some reason, I've always liked to sleep with the TV on as backroom noise. Something that is actually very common, although experts recommend against it. Unfortunately I haven't had a TV in the bedroom for some time. Although I may have missed this part out, a couple of times I have struggled to sleep, I've gone into the living room, laid on the sofa and stuck the tele on. Both times it's managed to help me drift off.

(Thank you American Office). Why not try then? I had already been down the road of white noise and pink noise, both were ineffective to me. Maybe the TV was my answer and definitely my most expensive step so far but one I had to take. I bought a 32" screen television and plonked it in the corner if my bedroom. The aim of this step was that whenever I couldn't sleep I would take out my ear plugs and watch TV, in the hope it would help me drift off. Not only was I hoping that it would get me to sleep but it seemed much less depressing actually watching something when wide awake in bed, rather than being laid there angry at the world. Just like most of my previous steps, this one had a promising start. The first time I tried it, I was asleep within 20 minutes, eventually waking up a few hours later, turning the TV off and drifting back to sleep. However it worked once and only once. After this I was finding myself trying to sleep with the TV on. Which is different to falling asleep with the TV on. It seems once again, I think I might have already mentioned it? My mind had beaten me.

The reason TV is not recommended by experts to help you sleep is the blue light exposure. Blue light is very damaging to sleeping patterns and should be avoided close to bed time, more about this in the next side chapter. However, many people fall asleep watching TV and although the obvious blue light exposure is not ideal, it is arguably the most effective

49

tool at distracting the brain from forcing yourself to sleep. Hence why it could be worth a shot, for people with insomnia, unfortunately though there's always a risk that watching TV laid in bed can further damage your sleeping pattern. Which is why I would say that pink noise and white noise are definitely the more preferred route and both of these should be trialled before turning to television.

Conclusion: Pink noise and white noise are the most recommended types of noise for people who're struggling with insomnia. They are, in fact, so well thought of that most sleeping apps will have white/pink noise as their main methodology for combatting insomnia. I would certainly recommend trialling both. If neither work then you could try television. Pretty much every expert would always tell you not to watch TV in bed as it can actually worsen insomnia. However due to the fact that it's incredibly effective as a distraction method and helps millions worldwide fall asleep, it could help. You'll have to assess your own personal situation as we're all different, for most TV is a bad idea but for some, it could be a great one.

PHONES, BLUE LIGHT AND BEDROOM ACTIVITIES

The TV wasn't my smartest idea to have in the bedroom. As I mentioned there are lots of people who opt to sleep with the TV on, whereas for me I feel it might have made me worse. Going back to the great Hugh Selsick now and listening to what he said on the subject really opened my eyes. He mentioned, on a podcast, that you should spend as little time in bed as possible and you should only ever be in bed to sleep or to have sex.

For me, I had been one of these people that liked to go on my phone in bed before I go to sleep, for half an hour or so. I also liked to work on my laptop in bed for a few hours some mornings. These are very poor practices. Watching TV, being on your phone, laptop, reading or anything that engages the brain, should not be done in bed. Doing so can trick your brain into associating these activities with being in bed and therefore once you're in bed for sleep, your brain could switch on. It took me a while before I realised this and who knows this could have been a trigger for my insomnia. Again though it's horses for courses. Some with sleeping problems have touted reading as the cure for their problems, whereas others it could worsen the situation. When it comes to blue light, especially mobile phones, I would find it hard to believe there's anyone on the planet that benefits in sleep from blue light.

People are gradually becoming more aware of the damage blue light can cause to sleep. It's almost common knowledge now that using your phone directly before you go to bed can be harmful to your sleep. In basic terms; the light from your phone tricks your brain in to thinking it's day time and thus your sleep issues can occur. In other terminology: blue light restrains the amount of melatonin our body produces, melatonin is naturally produced by the body and is produced at night to get you to sleep. It's also the same with blue light from your television. However with your TV, it will be generally be situated a much further distance from your eyes, rather than holding a phone in your hand. This makes it slightly less of a hinderance. The next question that often follows from this is; what time should you put down your phone and turn the TV off before bed? The general census is that you should go off your phone 1 hour before bed time. The national sleep foundation actually suggests that this time should be around 30 minutes. However, other sleep professionals like to suggest that being on your phone, unlike watching TV, needs a certain level or focus and alertness, hence the 1 hour suggestion. Meaning ideally you should be off your phone/laptop/ipad 1 hour before bedtime and the TV should be off 30 minutes before bed.

It's not just necessarily turning it off before bed that can help you sleep better though. Changing the brightness of your screen can also have an impact on sleep. Even better than just changing your brightness, you can actually apply blue light filters to modern day phones. With an iPhone you'll need to enter your display and brightness section in settings, go to night shift and move it more warm. This should lessen the blue light that your phone gives off. If you have an android phone go into settings > display, you can actually toggle on to apply a blue light filter constantly. Moreover there are apps that you can download to have a constant blue light filter on your phone. I'm not too sure if these cost and how effective they actually are, so be sure to do some research before just jumping in. The blue light filters available may not be as effective as they mention and it can still cause sleep issues with them on. Hence why the obvious best thing to do would be to restrict your phone use as much as possible.

One more key point to note with phone use, which many don't even consider, not only should you go off your phone 30 minutes before bed but also when first waking up. Just as our body clock naturally calms us down and helps us sleep at night, it will naturally help you wake up in the morning. Turning your phone on first thing and exposing yourself to blue light is going to damage your bodies natural routine and have a negative effect on your sleep. Stay off your phone first thing in the morning, last thing at night and restrict use throughout the day, it can do wonders for your sleeping pattern. Not to mention the benefits that these practises could have on your mental health. Which in turn, again will give you a much better chance of sleeping well at night.

As for other bedroom activities, it's simple. Do not use your bed for anything other than sleep or sex. Don't read in bed, watch TV, eat, drink or anything. In fact you should be spending as little time in bed as possible. Yes, that sounds completely counterintuitive but if you want better sleep, spending less time in bed is actually such a game changer. Most people will try and go to bed earlier to allow themselves more time to try and get some sleep before work. However, going to bed later, when you're more tired, will help you get better sleep. Going to bed too early may be when we aren't tired enough to sleep and then we'll leave ourselves frustrated and the insomnia will take control. For most people the first 30 minutes or so in bed are crucial. If you fail to fall asleep in this timeframe, you'll begin to doubt if you can sleep at all. Then the insomnia ensues. Hence why experts will normally tell you to start spending less time in bed than your current routine. More on this later on.

Conclusion: Restrict phone use and don't use it just before bed or first thing in the morning. Only use your bed for sleep and sex, nothing else. All this combined can be a great way to mentally help your sleeping pattern.

BREATHING TECHNIQUES

Fact: Everyone dreams every night and almost everyone will wake up during the night, every night. However some will remember and others won't. Hence why you may feel tired in a morning but think you slept all the way through the night.

I'm not sure how it is for most people that have insomnia but I know for myself, I would often spend the nights I can't sleep researching online 'how to sleep'. One technique that kept popping up was the relaxing thoughts idea. They tell you to lay there close your eyes, think of a relaxing image, something like a calm lake or beach is what they recommend. On top of this they'l tell you to count or focus on your breathing. Good luck with that. Anyone who suffers with insomnia will probably find this laughable. I wish to god at 3am I could switch my mind to think of a nice calm river instead of worrying about getting up in 4 hours time. There's not a chance a chronic insomnia sufferer can benefit from 'happy thoughts'. Well, not in my eyes anyway.

However breathing and routine patterns could be a viable option for sleepless nights. Patterns and techniques are used by the military and extreme adventurers who may need to sleep in terrible conditions. I decided to try a few different techniques, breathing patterns and thought processes. Out of several different methods I hit the one worked. Lord behold. Insomnia is finally defeated. This breathing and thought process technique was in fact the only one that I had found to have any effect whatsoever, after trialling 6 or 7.

At 4 in the morning it worked almost instantly, quicker than a sleeping tablet, it felt like an anaesthetic it worked so fast. I tried it again then a few days later when struggling to sleep and well, it worked again, perfectly. That's when I decided to put it into my normal everyday routine. Every night in bed I did this routine and it seemingly worked without falter. It goes as follows.

Lay in your bed, flat on your back and close your eyes. Next allow all of your muscles to relax one by one. Firstly think about your feet, toes and legs, allow them to completely relax and sink in to the mattress. Then do the same with your hips, stomach, arms, shoulders, neck and finally the head. This should significantly calm yourself down and allow to relax, your whole body softening. Once your muscles are relaxed take a deep breath in and change your thought process. On the article I read it said to think about a happy place but as mentioned earlier, for me, that's impossible. Instead of a happy place though, it says you can tell yourself over and over again in your head 'don't think'. I have no clue, not a single idea, (as I have already mentioned I am not a doctor nor a therapist) but for some reason this just works. Over and over again in my head 'don't think, don't think, don't think, don't think, don't think'. Gradually I feel myself drift away and next thing I know, I'm waking up.

No chance I was jumping the gun with this though. Every other technique I've tried that's worked, I get my hopes up and before you know it, back to square one. I kept this a secret and didn't want to tell anyone I thought I had solved my problems, at the worry I would jinx it. Then it happened, as you may be able to work out for yourself, with the pattern of the book so far, this method unfortunately didn't last forever. Again it lasted for a fortnight or so. Until 1 night I laid in bed 'don't think, don't think, don't think'. It went on and on and on. After what felt like 10 hours I checked my phone and I had been in bed for 40 minutes. Now this technique was torn apart. Next time I get into bed and follow the full step-by-step plan, 'don't think, don't think....', I knew it wasn't full-proof and therefore my mind would stay on overdrive. Unfortunately for me this breathing technique had become usless.

It was something expected now from self-experimentation. Experts will often try to teach you to change your thought processes at night and get yourself into a steady breathing pattern. Some may even try the technique I have mentioned above or something very similar. My mind and insomnia, though, overthinks to the point in which changing my frame of mind becomes very difficult. I believe this to be the case with most severe insomnia sufferers. Hence why the 'don't think' seemed to be the only one that at had any relative effect but unfortunately it didn't last. Breathing patterns and changing your thought process though have been proven to work for rough sleepers. Not only working for insomnia sufferers but also working for those sleeping in difficult surroundings. This is why I believe breathing patterns are definitely worth a shot as a fix for your insomnia battle. I would recommend that you try the above approach first but there are dozens online which you can trial.

Conclusion: Breathing patterns can work for insomnia but it's no guarantee. There are dozens of different breathing methods available online, which is why I recommend to trial them all, to see if any give you a positive effect.

VITAMINS

Fact: The COVID pandemic increased the number of insomnia sufferers vastly. In January 2021 Google saw a massive jump in UK search volume of the phrase 'How to sleep fast', being searched a total of 10,000 times in a month! A majority of these searches coming between 1am and 4am.

Thanks to the COVID pandemic I became aware of another completely different approach to insomnia. In an article written by a sleep expert he claimed that one of the main reasons people struggle to sleep is lack of vitamins. Which is a completely different concept to how most would treat insomnia. However I see it as something 100% worth experimenting on, as if all I had to do was take vitamins to sleep, how could I not try?

Firstly, ever since the pandemic has began people have been told to stay at home and not go to work, whilst they get paid some of their wages from the government. This will more than likely throw people's bodies out of sync and can lead to insomnia. Secondly, the amount of stress caused from the pandemic could be leading to sleepless nights for some people. With worries of uncertainty around jobs and the worry of possibly catching a deadly virus, you can understand how this would keep people up all night. Moreover it could even be a symptom of long covid. Again this isn't 100% correct and it'll take time and research to be sure but it seems absolutely possible. In fact many are already quoting insomnia as a direct symptom of long covid, which seems likely due to correlation of insomnia and covid cases. Whatever the reason is for insomnia cases increasing alongside covid cases, it's happening and people need to start getting the correct help.

The article I had read was actually found in a British newspaper, in which they got a sleep expert to write pieces during the COVID pandemic. It contained a 2 page piece on insomnia and the covid relation. In this piece they explained how the correlation is occurring and the possible reasons why. They then went on to give options of methods to try for better sleep. The options included things such as exercise, warm bath, no caffeine after 2pm and a whole list of others. All of which we have run through already and if you're still struggling at this point, none of them must have worked. However there was one other method that stood out to me and that was vitamin deficiencies. Essentially their claim is that having inadequate amounts of certain vitamins during the day can effect our bodies natural cycle. Now, if this is true, which it seems more than feasible, then this would definitely effect our sleeping pattern. For this though I wasn't optimistic. My diet had been very similar for years and I don't see how all of a sudden I wouldn't be getting enough of certain vitamins. I researched it though. Firstly I was anxious about taking a vitamin supplement which I already get plenty of via my diet. I wondered if you could actually overdose on vitamins. After plenty of research, it showed it's extremely difficult to take too much of a certain vitamin to the point it becomes damaging to the body. Therefore supplementing any vitamins should be fine. I then looked into multivitamins. Multivitamins seemed like a very simple way of 'covering all bases' so to speak. Researching into multivitamin's it became a common trend that many recommend against them. It's actually preferred if you try and figure out which vitamin or vitamins your diet doesn't provide enough of. Then supplement just that specific vitamin or vitamins. Multivitamins are very small amounts of any number of vitamins. Therefore you may still not get enough of the vitamin you need, whilst getting more of vitamins you don't need.

My next step then was to try and figure out what, if any, vitamins my diet didn't provide me with enough of. To do this I took note of my average diet and researched into how much of each vitamin my diet supplies. Not an easy process but it was quite interesting to see what I'm missing out on and I would recommend anyone to look for themselves. The only vitamin that popped up for me of being insufficient would be vitamin D. All the others I had in abundance. I mean I didn't check every possible vitamin and mineral there is but from my research, I checked the most essential.

This is the interesting part and something that seems uncommon knowledge. There are numerous experiments that have proven or as a minimum shown strong signs that show a vitamin D sufficiency could be linked to sleep problems.

Here's a direct quote from,

https://www.ncbi.nlm.nih.gov;

An intervention study reported that vitamin D supplementation (D3) in veterans (50,000 IU/week) increased their sleep duration [56]. Another double-blind clinical trial showed use of vitamin D supplementation (50,000 IU/fortnight for 8 weeks) facilitated sleep duration and quality in people with sleep disorders.

Moreover there are other experiments that have seen a correlation in melatonin and vitamin D. The evidence from these studies shows that a vitamin D insufficiency can directly relate to the body producing melatonin. As we've previously mentioned melatonin is an essential chemical, naturally produced in our body, which helps us relax and get to sleep. Combining all of this knowledge, it looks highly likely that a lack of vitamin D could lead to sleep problems and possibly insomnia. Take into the fact that this was the vitamin that my diet doesn't contain much of, could it be a massive coincidence? To me it seems like lack of vitamin D could be a major cause of my chronic insomnia.

Then I went on I ordered some vitamin D tablets offline and we were good to go. I mean maybe it's me being apprehensive to think that just taking 1 little tablet a day can completely cure a mental illness. Always worth a try though. I specifically remember the first night of supplementing vitamin D, I slept for roughly 8 hours. Sleeping for 8 hours to me is completely unheard of, I would say it only occurs a handful of times throughout an entire year, even pre-insomnia. Then I genuinely thought to myself 'I've cured insomnia and I'm going to be able to sleep better than I ever have before'.

The days went on and genuinely I was sleeping amazingly. Each night hitting around 6.5 -7.5 hours which is arguably my optimal sleep time. I managed to clock a full week in my sleep diary in which I slept a minimum of 6.5 hours every single night, insane. On the 8th night, just as with every other single method I've tried, reality hit me straight back. On the 8th night I had a terrible dose of insomnia, hitting a lovely total of 0.0 hours of sleep. Yes, there is significant evidence that shows vitamins, especially vitamin D, can be significant in getting good quality sleep. On the other hand you may have to question how effective they are when most top experts don't cover them whatsoever, when talking about insomnia. Although if just supplementing a tablet each day is going to give you even a 1% better chance of beating insomnia, then it seems worth it to me.

Moreover it's not just vitamin D either, that can help with sleep. Having an imbalance or insufficient amount of any vitamin or mineral can effect your sleeping pattern. Hence why I would recommend you to do some research into your own diet. Simply note down what you eat every day during a 1 or 2 week period. Firstly check if you any have sleepless nights alongside your eating diary. You may notice that each time you have a sleepless night you may be eating or aren't eating foods that you do on the days you sleep. This could be an obvious sign of what's triggering your insomnia. Moreover, once you have your diet written down you'll be able to look into your vitamin intake. Research into the foods you eat and note down how much of each vitamin you're getting on an average day. Then look into how much of each vitamin you should be consuming per day and you may notice some insufficiencies. Start to supplement on any vitamins that you're not getting enough off and you could see a big sleep improvement.

Conclusion: Vitamins more than likely won't be the full cure for your chronic insomnia. However it will definitely help towards the cure and I would highly recommend supplementing to anyone with insomnia. Not to mention that supplementing vitamins could have other benefits on your health and mental well-being.

SLEEP COCKTAIL

Fact: Experts say you should be cruising to dreamland within 10 to 20 minutes of your head hitting the pillow. If you fall asleep within five minutes, you may be sleep deprived; if it takes more than 20 minutes, this is a sign of insomnia.

Vitamins and minerals are incredibly brilliant and effective in dictating how our body works. As science progresses experts are discovering exactly how the brain works and what different chemicals or minerals we can supplement to change our way of thinking. There's a fantastic podcast by Andrew Huberman who will often talk about how different supplements can effect different parts of our brain. Surely then there must be supplements we can take to help sleep? Well we've just gone through vitamin D, vitamin D has been proven by double blind studies to have a positive effect towards sleep. However the studies are small and the overall evidence of vitamin D on sleep is minimal.

Another common supplement to take for sleep is melatonin. Melatonin is naturally produced in our bodies at night, which is the chemical that basically put; will help you feel sleepy and drift off. Hence why many people are now beginning to supplement with melatonin at night, for a sleep aid. Unfortunately, though, it comes with a few negatives, that make melatonin a bad idea for sleep. Firstly it can become habit forming. Just like with sleeping tablets if you become so used to the melatonin supplement, it will be a necessity rather than an aid. Eventually you may reach a stage of not being able to sleep without melatonin supplementation. Moreover melatonin is naturally produced by the human brain. Supplementing melatonin combined with the melatonin naturally produced could prove to be too much. These aren't the only reasons not too supplement melatonin. Evidence suggests that although melatonin can help us get to sleep, it's pretty useless at keeping us asleep. Most people that supplement melatonin will often get to sleep well but struggle to stay asleep, waking up regularly through the night. Taking all of this into consideration, I definitely do not recommend anyone to supplement melatonin for sleep.

Fear not though, as the chapter name suggests, there are a cocktail of supplements you can take said to be a game changer for insomniacs. Again taken from Andrew Huberman, he has designed a 3 supplement cocktail that he's claimed will help even the worst of sleepers get a good nights kip. What is in this cocktail then? Magnesium Threonate, Theanine and Apigenin. Taking this cocktail of supplements is going to help shut off the part of your brain which is responsible for anxiety, stress and over-thinking. All of which are common culprits for triggering insomnia. Now, supplementing 3 different products consistently is blatantly going to come at a price. A price of which will depend on where you buy your supplements and which brand you go for. I must reiterate though, as I'm sure anyone would agree, being laid awake at 4am, a few hours from you alarm, having been unable to sleep all night, there's not much of a price that would seem too extreme. Therefore even if it just helps slightly, I would definitely say it's worth it.

Again using myself as a guinea pig, I began taking this cocktail of supplements. All of which I attained from Amazon. It's recommended that the supplements be taken around 30-60 minutes before bed time. This should give enough time for the supplements to gradually take effect and allow you to drift off easier. The first night of trying this cocktail I did sleep extremely well, though the night before I had barely managed a wink so it was inevitable. It continued to work and I must say, whether it's a placebo effect or genuine, you can almost feel your brain stop to stress and overthink. Which then allowed me to fall asleep much easier. It worked consistently for roughly 10 nights before coming unstuck. Unfortunately I hit a bad patch and after 10 good nights sleep on the cocktail, it took little to no effect on my sleep. What was a concern for me was that it didn't work at all. I had a night of 0 minutes sleep and the reason I was awake was through my usual sleep anxiety. The whole point in this cocktail was to rid me of the anxiety that would trigger my insomnia but it had failed (on this occasion). However I felt enough promise from earlier nights to continue with my consumption of this cocktail, along with vitamin D.

There are a few pointers about this supplement cocktail that need to be noted before you consider taking it. Firstly the supplements themselves are healthy and safe, I feel like this needs to be made clear. However, as always, I would recommend consulting your doctor before the regular consumption of these supplements.. Looking at the individual supplements themselves though, they're all supplements that can have benefits which don't just include better sleep. Magnesium for example is a mineral that many people don't get enough of. Supplementation of this can help better functions of the body, as well as sleep improvements. Apegenin is very effective at stress relieving and is often found in chamomile tea. Whereas theanine is an amino acid that is said to help improve overall mental function. All of these points are viable reasons for taking each supplement, before you ever consider the sleep benefits.

As with most methods though, we have the bad and the good. With this cocktail of supplements, like most people, the first thing you think of is money. Consistently taking 3 different supplements over long periods of time is going to come at a cost. It's down to the individual as to whether they believe the cost to be worth it. Although as previously mentioned, once you've had consistent sleepless nights for a period of time, you become more than willing to stretch your wallet for a solution. The other negative is habit forming. Andrew has spoke about on his podcast that he believes it not to be habit forming at all and he certainly is the expert on this subject. For me though I believe anything can become habit forming. For someone who doesn't suffer from insomnia maybe it doesn't and they can come on and off the supplements as they please, with little consequence. For someone who suffers with insomnia it could become a mental dependance. Although your body may not need the cocktail to sleep, mentally you may believe that you need it. Thus making it hard to fall asleep without and it could become quite troublesome. Either way there's no evidence or experiments to back up either argument.

Conclusion: Supplementing magnesium threonate, apegenin and theanine before bed can help reduce anxiety to allow you a good nights sleep. I would highly recommend it for anyone to try and it could be a permanent fix. If not I would still recommend to use it for giving you a greater chance for sleep.

CAFFEINE, SUGAR AND DIET

Fact: According to a survey, in 2021, almost half of the UK have problems getting to sleep once a month or more. That's around 30 million people each month struggling not to sleep!

This leads on very well from the last chapter. What we put into our bodies is always going to be the maker of us. Eating different foods can make us gain or lose weight, cause or help depression, cause or reduce fatigue and of course effect our sleep. In the last 2 chapters I spoke about vitamins and various supplements, how I used them to see if they could cure my insomnia. Although they didn't completely cure me, I felt encouraged enough to continue supplementing vitamin D. I also felt encouraged to continue with my sleep cocktail. Which I still do to this day and more than likely will do for the foreseeable future. Vitamins aren't the only thing you can ingest that will effect your sleep. There's also many different foods and drinks that will have a positive or negative impact on your sleep. Hence why for this next step I decided to concentrate more on my diet and caffeine intake to see if it may help. My thoughts were that if just vitamins could help sleep problems, surely looking at my entire diet and nutrients could help even further. This is also another common step spoken about by many different sleep experts. (When first meeting a sleep therapist with insomnia, they'll often query your diet as there could be some glaring dietary mistakes that will lead to poor quality sleep.)

Firstly caffeine. Caffeine is a stimulant that is very common place in diets for a majority of adults across the world. Caffeine is also known to be a strong stimulant. A stimulant can be considered anything that increases alertness and energy in the body. Popular drinks containing caffeine are coffee, tea and energy drinks. All of these contain a considerable amount of caffeine and will make you feel more alert after drinking. It doesn't take a rocket scientist to realise that anything causing you to be more awake and alert is going to effect our sleep. For me, I very rarely actually drink anything containing caffeine so I highly doubt this would be the cause of my insomnia. It has been an issue though for me in the past and I've suffered from sleep issues for many years.

During my younger years I began taking a pre-workout supplement before the gym, which would be around 4:30pm. My sleep became very disturbed and more often than not it was taking me hours to get to sleep at all. Safe to say I ditched the pre-workouts pretty quick and my sleep returned to some sort of normality. This goes to show how easily caffeine can negatively hurt our sleeping patterns.

I decided to self-experiment once again with caffeine and started tracking my daily intake. I would generally have a coffee in the mornings once or twice per week. However if I had a sleepless night I would have to down 2 or 3 the following day just to survive. On the days I took coffee for enjoyment or a little kick, rather than survival, I wanted to see if this would directly correlate to insomnia. Once again looking back to Dr. Hugh Selsick, the sleep guru, he suggests that you should not have caffeine after 2pm. Caffeine has a half life of around 5 hours, meaning if you take a double espresso at 5pm you could still have a single espressos worth of caffeine in your body at 10pm. I took it one step further and decided I would only ever have caffeine as a coffee first thing in the morning around 8am, never any time after, unless after a sleepless night. My results showed there was 0 correlation between what nights I couldn't sleep and what days I took my morning coffee.

Next up I had to trial other methods in which my diet may be the issue. Firstly was sugar, sugar is another method of providing high energy and hyperactivity, again something that can be very damaging to sleep. For this reason I stopped eating any high sugary foods/drinks within a few hours of bedtime. Yes that meant no desserts after dinner, which also worked out well for improving my diet, like killing 2 birds with 1 stone.

Fact: Studies have found that people who eat high sugar/carbohydrate diets may fall asleep quicker than those who don't. However their sleep quality won't be as good and they're more likely to wake up multiple time during the night.

The next way in which diet can affect sleep is eating too much before you go to bed. As far as I'm aware there's no full-proof study to suggest eating too much at night will damage sleep. However for most people it's just how they understand their body. For me I love eating and I don't think there's a minute of the day I don't feel hungry or can't eat. Due to this I've been known to cave in a fair amount of food late at night. Bad idea. Every time it leaves me feeling bloated and hot in bed, which will quite often keep me awake. This not only occurs for me but a majority of people will find the same issues. Eating large amounts of food and then laying horizontal has been proven to cause indigestion, which again can keep you awake. However it's tricky. Studies show that being too hungry before bed can also make it harder for you to fall asleep. It's never simple is it? Finding the right balance is the key for this one. You don't want to go to bed too hungry nor do you want to go to bed too full. How do we find that perfect balance?

Experimenting. Work with your diet around eating at night and try to find that balance. It's an impossible answer for me to give as our bodies are all designed differently. For me personally, I normally have my dinner around 3-4 hours before bed time. Then around 1 hour or so before bed I'll have a few tablespoons of cottage cheese. This may seem extremely weird but cottage cheese is full of casein protein and an ideal food to eat before bed. This routine works for me in terms of diet, as I go to bed reasonably not hungry (even though I'm always hungry) and not too full that I feel like I can't roll onto my side.

These are 3 key examples which you can change in your diet and it will help you get better sleep. Clarifying these 3 steps;

Try to lower your caffeine intake to a reasonable amount and avoid caffeine after 2pm. Depending on your bed time but all in all try and avoid caffeine within around 7 hours of bed.

As with caffeine we have the same for sugar. You should really keep your sugar intake low anyway just for health benefits but now you have another reason too and that's to help you sleep. Moreover you should try and avoid eating/drinking sugar within a few hours of bed time.

As for how much you are eating, this too can have an impact on your sleep. For the best part you should avoid eating too much before bed and refrain from eating a big meal within a few hours of bed time. You also don't want to be too hungry when you go to bed, as this can cause issues with getting to sleep. Experiment with different timings and foods in the lead up to bedtime, until you find your ideal routine.

For a final 4th way in which diet may effect your sleep, we have our mental health. Again studies have show that eating an u unhealthy, high-calorie diet can have a detrimental affect on our mental health. Our mental health is just as important as our physical health. Having poor mental health is one of the key factors that will often crop up in insomniacs. It's what will lead us to stress and anxiety, in turn causing us to overthink and thus the sleep struggles will occur.

Conclusion: Caffeine, sugar and diet all have an impact on sleep. It only takes a few simple tweaks to help get better sleep. Not only can it help us sleep but changing our diets is a great way for helping us lead happier, healthier lives.

BED TIMES AND ROUTINE

Fact: According to a survey around 26% of adults in the UK say getting more sleep is a health ambition of theirs. More than half of these though say they're yet to put any steps in place for this.

The steps so far have been very much 'physical' steps. Although insomnia is much more mental, we can fix it by simple physical methods. Hence why these are the recommended route before diving much deeper.   After-all changing our mental processes aren't a simple fix and should only be used when absolutely necessary. The next step now is almost part physical and part mental. Changing our bed times and routines is very much a physical step and is a simple, effective method. Whereas the results we get from changing our bed times and routine can be much more mental.

It's also now got to a point where I have given up on my own journey and decided I need medical help. Unfortunately well not unfortunately, it's actually down to my own incompetence, I'm not currently signed up to a doctors. I'm very much a type of person that will avoid the doctors if possible and try to fix problems myself (as you can tell) or hope that they just fix themselves. Which has led me to not transferring doctors since I moved up to Newcastle from Grimsby, somewhat 2 years ago. Today I've printed the sign up forms off, I then have to fill them in and email a scanned copy to the doctors. After which I can't book an appointment for 48 hours but seeing as it's a Wednesday and a long weekend, it will take a week. Annoying and frustrating but I actually feel relieved that I'm taking steps towards proper treatment. This will also help with future research, as although I have in-depth knowledge from books, podcasts and websites, a doctor will provide me with much more personalised information.

This week so far I've slept soundly. Granted it's only Thursday now but it makes it a total of 5 normal sleeps on the bounce for me. Which is rare these days. The last few days I've tweaked up my routine and my bed time. Once again this is a Dr. Hugh Selsick method and something that I have already spoken about previously in the book. Most people when they struggle with sleep will start going to bed earlier. Thinking that the longer you're in bed the better chance you'll have of getting good sleep. It's actually the complete opposite. Ideally you want to spend less time in bed so that when your head hits the pillow you're ready to go to sleep. Going to bed too early will have you struggling to sleep straight away and the insomnia cycle begins. Due to this I have decided to knock my bed time back an hour. This will have me in bed for exactly 8 hours. Meaning after deducting wake ups and time getting to sleep, I should, in theory, still manage 7 hours sleep. It will be tough as on the days I don't sleep, the next day I can barely keep my eyes open past 8/9pm. However I'm more determined than ever to conquer my insomnia.

There's also another couple of other alterations you should be making to your sleep routine. Similarly to what I began to do. Firstly I wanted to start making sure I don't go to sleep until I'm tired. Ideally attempting to go to sleep at the exact time every night but I know some nights I won't feel tired at the same time. This generally occurs on a Sunday night, for me, as it's when my body is out of routine or if I play football late on and I feel pumped up til late in the night. Therefore, just make sure that you are feeling tired before you decide to hit the hay. Hopefully that'll stop the flustered laid in bed feeling, when maybe you're not even tired enough to sleep. This is almost a milder version of the technique known as 'sleep restriction'. Sleep restriction is one of the most effective methods for insomnia, used in chronic cases by top experts. However we may not need to implement sleep restriction completely and for now I recommend just trying to go to bed later than usual, making sure you aren't going to bed until you feel 100% ready for sleep.

Finally you should try to keep this up on weekends. Similarly to most adults, especially in the UK, I like to drink on a weekend and will normally be up later than usual. Which makes it more than difficult to keep up my bed and get up times on a weekend. I'm also not a robot and want to enjoy myself, without letting insomnia take over my life completely. However sometimes you just have to make sacrifices in life to get where you want to be. This included with insomnia, forcing yourself to stay in or go home earlier than usual on a weekend could put you on the right path to being cured. I will reiterate this won't last forever. Eventually when you have fixed your insomnia, you won't have to worry as much about going to sleep at 4am on a Saturday or sleeping in till 11am on a Sunday. For now, though, you need to implement this strategy.

These are the exact methods in which I decided to implement in my own routine. It's well-documented that going to bed and getting up at the same time is very important to establish a good sleeping pattern. Moreover, experts have implemented later bed times for people with insomnia for many years now. We should only be in our beds when we're completely ready to fall asleep, then when we wake up we should get out and not get back in bed until we're again ready for sleep. Genuinely, just giving yourself a better routine and less time in bed can have incredible results.

When I followed this method during self-experimentation, I would say it was the most effective at this point. In fact it shocked me at how quickly I saw benefits and how much it genuinely helped me. I had 1 sleepless night in 10 nights, cracking stuff! Moreover I started to actually feel well rested, as in I genuinely felt like this less time in bed is a life hack for me. I've always known I can live off less than 8 hours but assumed the more time I lay in bed the better and conclusively would get better sleep this way. Well I can certainly put that myth to bed, as living off 6.5 hours sleep, for me, was was definitely the optimal amount and still is.

Today also marks the day that I can now book a doctors appointment (at last). A week from today I have my doctors appointment and hopefully it will put me on the right path. My main aim is to convince the doctor that sleeping pills are not the way and I want to be referred for CBT (cognitive behavioural therapy). My doctor has prescribed me with 2 things. Firstly he's prescribed me with sleeping pills. Not what I wanted but it's only a small prescription and he's confident if I only use them a couple times a week, there's no chance of addiction. The aim is that hopefully they can kick me into a routine but I'm wary about taking them. Secondly he prescribed me a method known as sleep distraction and this is my next venture.

Conclusion: Bed times and routine is essential for good and proper sleep. Going to bed and waking up at the same time is going to align your body clock and your mental state. Not an out and out cure for insomnia but a huge step in the right direction.

MEDITATION

Fact: Randy Gardner has the record for longest time without sleep (without using drugs), it stands at 11 days and 15 minutes. He did it to try and prove that sleep deprivation isn't as damaging as people think. After the experiment he did a press interview were he spoke without slurring his words and seemed to be in excellent health.

Since going to pick up my tablets yesterday from the pharmacy, I was put onto a couple of other ideas to try from the pharmacist. 1 being CBD, which I have already experimented with and it didn't help my insomnia. Also doing some research I can see that links between CBD and helping insomnia are minimal. Number 2 on the list was meditation. Now I have flirted with meditation previously, aware of the benefits it can have on your mental health. However I've never been consistent and never managed to get to a point I feel it actually gives me much benefit at all. This time I'm going to remain consistent and see if meditation is another step towards the insomnia cure.

According to the sleep foundation, meditation is practised by around 1 in 6 Americans and has been found to help with sleep problems. Here's a direct quote from the sleep foundation.

Research suggests that various types of meditation can help improve insomnia, and may even improve sleep quality for those without existing sleep problems. Mindfulness meditation, in particular, appears to improve sleep quality and reduce daytime disturbance in people with chronic insomnia and older adults. In the long term, these improvements may be comparable to effects seen from sleep medication or other established methods for insomnia treatment. Like other sleep treatments, a main goal of meditation is to take the pressure off to fall asleep.

If you aren't sure of what to make of this, it simply means that meditation is a tool used to help relax the mind and block out stressful thoughts. Stressful thoughts are often what keeps us awake so blocking them out will give us a greater chance of sleep. Not only this but meditation is said to be the key to inner peace. For many people the reason insomnia can occur is stress's and pressures from things such as work, relationships and financial issues. Meditation is going to help relieve stress and give our minds a gateway to mental peace. Which again, like other methods we've tried, is not only brilliant for insomnia but will lead you to a better life in general..

Let's look at how to meditate, as it's something I'm not very efficient at I imagine this to be somewhat of a learning curve. To begin with you're supposed to find somewhere peaceful and quiet, (already sounding difficult in my house hold). Then you need to get comfortable, either seated or laid down it doesn't matter but you need to be as comfortable as possible. When most people think about meditation they think of a monk sat on a rug with legs crossed and hands raises either side, looking like a salt bae hand, well that's not necessarily how it goes. The aim is to be as comfortable as possible, whether that be with legs crossed or straight out. You can be on the floor, a chair or a sofa it doesn't particularly matter. Then you need to set yourself a timer, some kind of alarm that will alert you but in a gentle manner. You don't want to be coming out of a peaceful meditation session with a siren blasting off in your ear. Try get a soothing alarm or something that even just softly vibrates. Set your alarm to however long you plan to meditate, although for beginners it's recommended around 5 minutes. Once you get used to meditating you can increase the time frame. Once the clock is set you can begin to meditate.

Start by closing your eyes and focus on your breathing. Breath slowly in and out, focus on each breath, think about the breathing, don't worry about the length of breath or if it's through your nose/mouth.

Just think about breathing in and then breathing out, nice and slow. Try to focus on your breathing and gradually other things will slip into your mind, don't worry it's supposed to happen. Once you realise you're no longer thinking about your breathing, try get back to it. Push your other thoughts to the side and focus on your breathing in and breathing out. These thoughts will continue occurring but don't worry it's natural. Some thoughts you'll wonder how it even came to your head but allow it to come and then push it aside. Don't beat yourself up if you struggle to concentrate on breathing at all, it's natural, the more you meditate, the more efficient you'll become. Once your timer goes off gradually come back. Slowly open your eyes and come back to the world. Don't worry if at first you don't feel much from it, it takes time and practise for meditation to work it's magic.

This is the method that I used for meditation. As for timing of the meditation, it's believed that meditating close to bed time is the best for insomnia. For me I'll meditate in the living room, laid on the sofa, just before I go to bed. Help myself drift into a state of calm and relaxation before heading to bed. I will not be meditating in my room, as we know that you should only be in bed for sleep and nothing else. I am also still going to bed at a later time so I spend less time in bed. On top of this I'm still supplementing vitamin d, having no caffeine and not going on my phone 1 hour before bed. In addition to the supplement cocktail I have before bed time. Now it's time to add 5 minutes of meditation before I hit the hay.

Last night was my first night experimenting with late night meditation. I found, when meditating, the urge of my thoughts to drift away were powerful, however , surprisingly I wasn't thinking about going to sleep. For insomnia sufferers, including myself, normally at night time the thought of 'will I sleep or not' slips into the mind like a burglar breaking into a home. Once in your mind you know you're in for a long night ahead. Fortunately this didn't happen for me and instead as my mind drifted it was to much more random thoughts about general life. As my mind would slip I would pull it back to my breathing and refocus. Although only a 5 minute window it felt like I had let my mind wander 100+ times but I stuck with it. It was just a constant battle of pointless thoughts, breath in and out, thoughts about work, breath in and out, thoughts about football, breath in and out. Then the strangest, craziest thing that could have happened, happened. I woke up! My alarm had gone off, my 5 minutes was over and I had slipped so deep that I had some how managed to fall asleep. If only it was in my bed and not my sofa but no complaints, I went to bed and fell asleep almost instantly.

Fast forward a week now and so far meditation has worked brilliantly. Some nights not as well as others but I'm hoping as I become more efficient, meditation will get easier and work better every time. As I've mentioned, meditation helps sleep by pushing the negative thoughts out of your mind, these negative thoughts can often be the cause of insomnia. For me it's helped by taking my mind off sleep. Although it doesn't completely clear my mind, I no longer think about sleeping as much.

I persisted with the meditation for some time. Roughly around 2 months which was significantly longer than I had done for other methods of self-experimentation. The reason for this is firstly that meditation helped vastly. I had all of a sudden stopped worrying so much about sleep and thinking of ways to cure insomnia, instead I just allowed the meditation to help ease away my sleep anxiety. Secondly was the fact that I knew meditation would become more effective over time. Even just after a matter of a few weeks I could feel myself becoming more efficient with meditation. My mind seemed to be more prepared for it and I was much more competent at concentrating on my breathing. This could be a factor of me becoming more efficient at meditation or it could just be down to me not have as many life stress's as previously.

Either way it was working better and better, however I'm still suffering from sleep issues.

I've now been meditating for around 7 weeks. I've also been taking zoplicone sleeping tablets on the days I have struggled to sleep. On average it's been around 2 or 3 tablets per week, some nights I've double dropped as the first didn't take enough effect. Hence why I'm now down to my last 2 pills and awaiting another doctors appointment. Next step will more than likely be therapy. As for meditation the evidence says for me that it hasn't worked. I'm still suffering from bad insomnia 2 or 3 nights per week, which is no improvement from before. As an insomniac if you try this method you may have the same issues. My issue being that my meditation calms me a little bit but not enough and as soon as my meditation is over my sleep anxiety kicks in. It can work though and is a method proven to help relieve stress and anxiety, becoming ever more popular and used by millions worldwide. Therefore if your insomnia is caused by stress and anxiety I would recommend meditation. Even if you believe your insomnia to be caused by something else, meditation can be a useful tool. Which is why I will continue to meditate for the foreseeable future and would recommend it to almost anyone.

Conclusion: Meditation is a proven method of helping relieve anxiety and stress. Anxiety and stress are 2 of

the most common culprits of causing insomnia. Therefore meditation can be another step to the insomnia cure. However don't beat yourself up if you struggle early on with meditation, stick with it and you'll be like a Shaolin monk in no time.

SLEEP DISTRACTION

Fact: The American Sleep Foundation states that you cannot train yourself to sleep on less. Although you may get by on less you want be functioning as well. It's believed that 80% of our need to sleep is genetic. Meaning if your parents get by on little sleep, It's more then likely you will be the same.

Here I am at the 1000th step of my journey it seems. I've just had a 2nd meeting with my doctor and we discussed what the next steps would be. Firstly he's told me that they can't prescribe any more sleeping tablets as it's a 1 off prescription, which I'm happy about. The next step we both agreed would be to see a therapist. To be more clear a cognitive behavioural therapist. In the UK we're lucky enough to have a free health service but sometimes that can hinder the service we get. My doctor has given me the number of a free therapy service close to home but he said the waiting list could be long. Something that I always expected but I've been suffering with insomnia for many months now and the sooner I get on a waiting list the sooner I get seen, even I have to wait. The other option would be to pay for a cbt, which is I suppose is a personal choice. Therapists are generally expensive

92

and not accessible for people who aren't on high wages. This will also relate to people in different countries who don't have the luxury of a free health service. This is also one of the main reasons I have wrote this book. Although I do not claim this book will help cure you more effectively than a high-quality therapist, it will go through all the steps that the therapist will also go through with you. Therefore it's a much cheaper alternative and I'm confident we can cure even the worse insomniacs. With my GP though he didn't just palm me off to get therapy, fortunately he actually gave me some incredible advice that is amazingly effective against insomnia . To begin with he reeled off every single thing I have already tried, to which he seemed quite amazed none had really helped at all. However he added one more step to follow, which he states works in many cases. Sleep distraction is the next play in the book. Sleep distraction is actually a method which I've stumbled across previously but never given the time of day. Well maybe not the think fact I hadn't given it the time of time but more the fact that I didn't like the sound of what it entailed. Hence why I tried other ways to fix my insomnia before going with the sleep distraction method.

Sleep distraction is when you get in bed and if for 20 minutes you haven't slept, you'll then get up and leave the bedroom for 20 minutes, before heading

back to bed. When you leave the bedroom, the idea is to distract your mind so you aren't thinking about sleep. The most ideal method of this is to read a book, you should try to avoid blue light. After 15-20 minutes of reading head back to bed and try again. You can repeat this over and over again, which could mean constantly getting out of bed every 20 minutes and reading, if necessary. This is a method that sleep experts will use on pretty much every single patient. Sleep distraction paired with other techniques will cure almost every insomnia patient in the world. Now, if you're wondering why this wasn't just the first step of the book, to save the hassle of previous steps. Well, simply put sleep distraction is a big step to take. Forcing yourself to consistently get out of bed through the night is tough and the only people willing to go through with it are people who've become somewhat desperate. Hence why we try milder steps to begin with. I mean would you rather just need a hot bath before bed to fall asleep or would you want to be constantly getting out of bed for 20 minute time slots? I know which one sounds easier to me.

This is another step that I'm going to try and will run concurrently with my wait for a therapist. There's no specific science of why this works but it's one of the top methods used by top sleep specialists. Hopefully it can be effective in distracting my brain enough so that you no longer think about insomnia. The idea is that if you haven't fallen asleep within 20 minutes your body might not be prepared yet to sleep. On average it takes 10-20 minutes for adults to fall asleep so if you miss that window you fall in the category of 'struggling to get to sleep'. For most people this can be normal and occur from time to time but for an insomniac this could mean you're in for a long night. Sleep distraction will not only help take your mind away from sleep anxiety but it will also get you out of bed. Being in bed for too long is a common cause of insomnia, staying in bed without sleeping is what will start the flustered, anxious cycle, thus leading to a sleepless night.

This was to be my next step then, although I will be speaking to a therapist for a consultation to plan my next steps. In the week waiting for my therapy consultation I've only had 1 night of difficult sleep. Maybe this is down to the meditation, later bed time and dietary changes made so far. Maybe it was just a good week for me. The night I struggled to sleep I used the sleep distraction method to try and force some sleep. Whenever I thought I had been a while in bed I would check the time time to see how long. If it was 20 minutes or over I would get out of bed walk into the living room and read a book for 15-20 minutes. This I would cycle continuously to try and break the insomnia. After many cycles and an abundance of reading, I did finally manage to nod off. For a rough total of 3-4 hours, which in insomnia language translates to a half decent nights kip. Successful first attempt in my eyes and tonight I have a consultation with my therapist to discuss further help.

Conclusion: Sleep distraction works. Although not concrete, it's a method taught by sleep experts as one of the key steps towards beating insomnia. I do think there's times when even leaving the bed, your thoughts will be of going back to bed, which may make it less effective. However it's a method that has been used for years and is pushed by general practitioners as well as sleep therapists, which definitely makes it an effective method.

CBT/ SLEEP RESTRICTION

Fact: Sleep debt exists. People often don't believe that catching up on sleep is a real thing but studies have proven it is. Depriving yourself of optimal sleep for some nights can gradually be made back up by more sleep the next. However if you're an insomniac this is an ill-advised method.

Now we have arrived to the final chapter of this section. If you have made it this far, then I can only assume that none of the steps have been enough for you either. It's better to take the smaller steps before getting to this stage, as we're now at a point of complete lifestyle changes. If you're already cured and just read on out of curiosity, then I'm happy we found your solution. The next step is CBT, cognitive behavioural therapy. The most extreme method of curing insomnia and only needed in the most severe cases. Unfortunately this is the stage which I needed and if you're yet to be cured, then it will be the same for you.

(I created this book to allow people access to effective insomnia treatment without the need of therapy. Although I have reiterated the importance of therapy. For me, I did go through therapy, in fact I genuinely had 3 separate therapists, as they struggle to help my issue. Incredibly whilst going through wait times and being passed around therapists, I actually cured myself of my insomnia. So much so that by the time I came to meet my third and final therapist, her guidance was something I had already implemented. Somehow I had managed to be one step ahead of the experts. The benefit of me going through this therapy process though mean I can now relay their methods in this book. It also gives me reassure to know the information I am providing is 100% legitimate, taught and used by professionals).

Again I'm using self-experimentation with this phase. Although CBT is almost the pinnacle of treatment for insomnia, I've always been somewhat apprehensive about how effective it could. I've never been one to believe just talking to someone about my issues can guarantee me a solution. Which is why I went in to CBT already doubting it.

Last night was my consultation phase. My consultation was taken with me and a therapist who specialised in CBT for insomnia. Throughout the session he just wanted to know every single detail of my insomnia. When it started, why it possibly started, how often it occurs, what type of insomnia I suffer from, what I've already tried and everything else you could possibly want to know. Firstly he stated that everything I've tried is the correct procedure and good steps to take. (Which was nice to get face to face confirmation from an expert). However when you suffer from chronic insomnia it's more of a mental health illness and therefore needs to be dealt with accordingly. When a majority of the steps so far have been physical, next we need to start working on our thought process. As with most therapists in the UK, there's a waiting list. Fortunately for me it's not too long to see a sleep specialist and I've been placed on the list.

The therapist I held a consultation with did give me some more advice though, another step towards curing my insomnia. It goes by the term sleep restriction. I've already spoken about the idea of spending less time in bed and being in bed for as little as possible. Perhaps I didn't take this as serious as I should have or go to big enough lengths with this method. Although I had started going to bed later, it turns out I should be going to bed even later. Hopefully you have been keeping a sleep diary, as I have mentioned you should do. Now roughly work out your average over a 2 week period. Figure out how much on average you sleep on a decent night, when you feel well rested the next day. For me it's 6 hours. With sleep restriction the target is to go to bed exactly that amount of time before your morning alarm. For example, if my alarm wakes me up at 7am, then I should be going to bed around 1am. It may seem a strange tactic, as generally it takes some time to fall asleep and most people wake up for brief periods through the night. Therefore going to bed 6 hours before your alarm will mean you're getting more like 5 or less hours sleep. This will be difficult to begin with and I must stress you should stick to this every night, even if you have barely slept the night before. This works as your body understands that it needs this amount of sleep. As you're gradually getting a little bit less every night, your body will start to fall asleep quicker. It's also a tactic that works with maintenance insomnia, which is people who have trouble staying asleep. Once getting into bed with only a small space of time for sleep, you're more likely to not wake up during the night. Hopefully after some weeks you'll hit a point of falling asleep within a few minutes of your head hitting the pillow, once you become more efficient at this. Meaning for me it would be the point in which I am consistently sleeping 6 hours from the minute my head hits the pillow. At this point I should then add 15 minutes on to my bed time. The aim is to consistently keep adding 15 minutes until you reach your optimal sleep time. Your optimal sleep time is dictated by whatever amount of sleep has you feeling at your best. However, this doesn't always have to be the way it's followed. It you follow sleep restriction and *believe that you hit your optimal sleep straight away, then just stick with these timings. This is my next step to try and I feel like it's another very strong step towards a chronic insomnia cure.*

Here's all you need to know about sleep restriction. Sleep restriction was invented by Arthur Spielman a psychology professor. It's one of the most effective procedures to treat any insomnia and used by sleep specialists worldwide. Once you set your average time, you need to make sure it's not less than 5.5 hours. Even if you sleep less than 5.5 hours, this is the minimum amount of time you can spend in bed. Once you are sleeping better and having minimal wake up time and minimal amount of time falling to sleep, you can increase time in bed by 15 minute increments. Once doing this you can gradually increase the time until you hit an ideal sweet spot. Keep in mind our sweet spot will all be different, don't feel as if you have to work up to 7 hours of sleep, instead work with your optimal sleeping pattern, which could be 6 hours or 8 hours. For this procedure to be correctly conducted you need to follow the pattern 7 days a week. Understandably people like to let their hair down more on a weekend, thus this could be difficult to continue. However as your time in bed will more than likely be a short slot, it shouldn't be too much of an issue. For this step it also has to be kept long term, it's not something you can expect to just follow for a few weeks and suddenly you're cured. Beating insomnia is a process, it takes time but I'm sure we can all agree, it's most definitely worth it.

Conclusion: Sleep restriction is the most commonly used tactic for beating insomnia. It's used by the best sleep experts across the globe and can be used for almost any case of insomnia. This is the most extreme step so far but definitely the one that should help chronic insomniacs. Although at first you may feel sleep deprived, as after bad nights sleep you'll be forcing yourself to stay awake. On top of this it may take you some time to get to sleep so the sleep deprivation could be worsened. It is, though, very effective and if you want your insomnia gone I suggest you stick with it.

THE 3 STEP PLAN TO BEATING CHRONIC INSOMNIA.

For me I have just finished my CBT course and although I had to transfer around different therapists it went well. Throughout this time I have carried on in-depth research, along with self-experimentation and specialist help.

Via all this I have managed to cure my own chronic insomnia and after a lifetime of bad sleep, I feel incredible for it. To this point I no longer have sleepless nights, I rarely have bad nights and if so, it's never sleepless. Now a bad night is 4 hours, which hasn't happened for a while and lets face it, it happens to even the best of sleepers occasionally. I look back on where I was before, in my deepest, darkest, most troublesome sleepless periods and wonder how I made it through. It's exhilarating to not worry about how I'm going to sleep on a day-to-day basis and instead have my focus on other aspects of my life. I've pinned it down to 3 big changes I've made. Lifestyle, sleep improvement methods and mentality. All 3 of these steps when worked on together, will provide the solution to even the worst of insomniacs. Each big change is made up of little steps/changes that compliment each other. It was an easy plan to devise, simply going from all scientifically proven evidence, what my specialist told me and my own experimentation I could pick out the key, most effective methods.

Now we're going to take it into the 3 step plan. Firstly it will be small lifestyle changes. These lifestyle changes are ones that improve sleep and give you a better chance of falling asleep. All of them are well-known and are used not just by insomnia sufferers but others who are attempting just to catch some extra winks each night. The next step is sleeping methods that are scientifically proven to help people with insomnia. Also the 2 main methods used by sleep specialists, this step will be focussing around the ideas of sleep restriction and sleep distraction. Finally our 3rd step of the plan, which is mentality. Mentality is essential when overcoming sleep problems. Insomnia is mainly created by our minds. That can be from working shift patterns, in which our minds can become confused of when we should be sleeping and when we should be awake. Moreover our mentality can cause us anxiety, stress, flustering, all which can lead to sleep problems. This is were we need to help ourselves mentally, have a better outlook towards sleep and using our minds we can alleviate some of them anxious thoughts that we have. Remember how powerful our brains are, we need to use it for better and stop letting it rule our lives.

LIFESTYLE

Changing our lifestyle can seem like a drastic step and something that ideally, we wouldn't have to go through. Changing our lifestyles to help insomnia though certainly isn't drastic and I think any long term insomnia suffer will echo my words in saying no step is too drastic by this point. During this phase it's not a complete lifestyle change at all. Instead it's slightly altering certain aspects of your life, which may be part of your sleep problems. It's also a step, which many specialists may not even put you through and instead go straight for a mental process. Well, certain parts of your lifestyle are scientifically proven to help with sleep.

Just subtle alterations to your diet and routine can have a huge impact on how you're sleeping at night. Although it may not be the full, complete cure, it's certainly a great foundation. We will also work on some techniques that may be the cause of your insomnia. Some people may want to dive straight into therapy, thinking they have a bad case of chronic insomnia. When actually they might just be having caffeine too late In the day, which is making them struggle to get to sleep and thus the insomnia cycle continues. Which brings us into our first small lifestyle change.

CAFFEINE

What is caffeine? Caffeine is a natural stimulant that is mostly found in tea, coffee and cacao plants. It provides a stimulus to the brain and central nervous system, which in turn allows you to feel more energetic and reduce the onset of tiredness. It's the worlds most commonly used drug and is unregulated in almost all parts of the world. This is exactly the reason why we need to be careful around our caffeine intake. Humans like to take caffeine to give them a feeling of alertness and help them power through tough days. Most of the time people will opt for caffeine in the morning and instead of beating the morning grogginess themselves, have the caffeine beat it for them.

Once the morning caffeine has worn off some will often feel fine as it's later on in the day and therefore carry on their day-to-day business caffeine free. Others may want little boosts of caffeine throughout the day, to keep them at that energised level. However caffeine can also become highly addictive, having a regular intake can lead your body to needing it, rather than wanting it. To put it basically; say the average person consistently runs at an energy level of 6/10. Once they drink a coffee their energy levels elevate to 8/10, making them much more energetic. As you become more dependent on caffeine, your body will naturally produce less alertness and depend more on caffeine to get you to an average level. Making someone who's addicted to coffee regularly running at an energy level of around 4/10 but a coffee may take them back up to the 6 level. Hence the dangers of caffeine addiction. As you become more tolerant your body needs more and more for that extra boost. Until eventually you're taking too much and endangering your health. This isn't definitive, I must add, many people can have multiple coffees throughout the day and lead a healthy life. You just need to be aware of the dangers around too much caffeine, as it can be something you slip into without realisation.

Caffeine for insomniacs has to be treated with extreme caution. In all honesty it comes down to; the less caffeine the better. Im fact if you could get by on your life with 0 caffeine then that would be the most ideal scenario. Something that's very possible, if you're willing to gradually take the caffeine intake down until you hit the point of 0. If not though, then you should only be taking caffeine in the mornings. Caffeine is said to have a half life of 4-6 hours. Meaning if you have a double espresso, then you can still have a full espresso in your system 6 hours later! The total life of caffeine in your system can last for up to 10 hours! This makes caffeine an extremely dangerous drug in terms of sleep. Considering it can stimulate your brain for up to 10 hours after intake, you need to be very weary of caffeine.

For this first step you need to cut down your caffeine intake to as little as possible, ideally cut it down to none. You should not take caffeine after 12pm, lunch time. This is a guideline for people who work the average 9-5 job. Others who work shifts, nights or later shifts, you should just avoid any caffeine 10 hours prior to bed time. If you need an extra boost to get you through the day then by all means go up to 8 hours before but 10 is the target for this step.

EXERCISE

Depending on what type of person you are, you'll either love the sound of this word or loath it. Exercise is such a basic method for helping people with sleep but it definitely helps. Going back as far as you can think, well into your younger years, you may recall your parents saying 'you'll sleep well tonight'. Often referring to the fact you've been running around manic all day, wearing yourself out. As we grow older though, this never changes. The more we move and exert energy throughout the day, the more tired we'll become physically and mentally, the more tired we become, the better chance of good quality sleep. Just like if you've ever had a pet dog.

They'll often have days running around the house like a spider trapped in a glass, they're just too pumped up of energy. Take them for a long walk and you can almost guarantee that within 10 minute of getting home they'll be asleep. Not only is exercise going to help sleep but it also has a mass of other significant health benefits. Exercise can help lose weight, improve general health, reduce chance of disease/illness and improve your mental wellbeing. All good reasons to take up regular exercise.

As we mentioned earlier in the book, studies have shown that physical exercise and sleep have a bidirectional relationship. Which basically means that they help each other going both ways. More exercise will help get better sleep, while getting better sleep helps you exercise better. In fact in the 2013 sleep in America poll, they found that for people who regularly exercise 76-83% of them have high quality sleep. For peopler that don't regularly exercise this number drops to 56%. Not only this but sleep also has a highly positive effect on our mental health. When we exercise our body releases chemicals called endorphins. Endorphins are powerful chemicals that benefit our mental well-being. Endorphins are very effective at reducing stress and depression. In fact exercise is said to be an effective underused method of treating mild to moderate depression. Stress, anxiety and depression can be direct causes of chronic insomnia.

For this step I recommend that you try to get 30+ minutes of exercise regularly. Aiming for 5 days per week. In total you should be trying to hit around 3 hours minimum of exercise each week. Others may want to workout more, as their bodies may be more accustom to a heavy workload. In fact, as you exercise more, you may also want to include longer sessions to help keep the body fatigued at night. Training for 30 minutes may begin difficult but over time your body will adapt and 30 minutes will become too little for a good workout. Upping the time and intensity is a great way to keep up with you developing body.

In terms of what exercise to do, almost any exercise is going to be beneficial. However higher intensity, more cardio based exercise will generally burn more calories and leave you feeling more fatigued after. This is why something a bit more sweaty is better for helping you drift off at night. This isn't for everyone though and if you just want to hit some heavy weight sessions then go for it. Just make sure whatever exercise you go for you're pushing yourself and burning calories.

Unfortunately it's not all as simple as 'exercise helps you sleep'. In fact sometimes it can be quite the opposite and be something that keeps you awake. As we workout adrenaline will pump through our bodies, adrenaline will increase mental focus and speed up your heart rate. It's a no-brainer that both of these are going to effect your ability to fall asleep. Hence why I recommend that you don't perform exercise within 3-4 hours of bedtime. In a perfect world you could exercise early in the morning and none of this would be applicable for you. For most people though we exercise when we can, around our work and life schedules. If you can, make sure that you finish exercise 4 hours before your head hits the pillow. If you have to finish 3 hours before, then you should still be on the safe side. Any less than this and your swimming in dangerous waters. When it comes to curing your chronic insomnia, you need to be willing to make significant changes to your lifestyle. If this means tampering with your workout regime, then it's got to be done.

DIET

Having a healthy diet is the complete foundations of living a healthy lifestyle. Not only can eating the right foods be a one way trip to good health but eating at the right times can also be key. This is the same when it comes to a good nights sleep. We need to make sure that we aren't eating certain foods and we aren't eating at bad times. Generally speaking we all recognise just after eating as a good time to fall asleep. Perhaps not on purpose but many of will often feel the need to drift off after a big meal or slump down into a comatose state after eating dinner. Well that's usually down to eating large amounts of carbohydrates. Although carbs are simply thought of as energy, to fuel our body, we'll often find that after a large carb based meal we begin to feel sluggish and sleepy. Moreover though, it doesn't always mean that we'll drift off to sleep but instead just feel lethargic. In fact maybe unable to sleep for feeling too full. This is not how we want our diets to be based around.

There's no definitive answer of when you should eat in relation to bed time. Studies have shown that going to bed too soon after eating can leave you in difficulty getting to sleep. However studies have also shown that going to bed too hungry can also have you struggling to sleep. Which makes you wonder, which is it? Well, it's a case of straight down the middle. You should be going to be not feeling full but also not feeling hungry. It's impossible to state an exact timescale of when you should stop eating or have your last big meal. We're all different when it comes to digestion of food and how quickly our bodies digest certain amounts of different foods. For a general rule of thumb I would say to not eat anything big within 4 hours of bed time. The trick here though is to play around with a few different eating routines in the evening and see which one you feel most comfortable with when hitting the hay.

Another important point to note is that you should be careful of too much refined sugar before bed. Things such as candy, chocolate, fizzy drinks etc can provide an energy spike, commonly referred to as a sugar rush. A sugar rush is something we encounter lots as children. Constantly chomping down on candy and chocolate until our teeth hurt or until a responsible adult pulls us away. Well when we hit adulthood we tend to forget the effects of sugar and the fact it can give us a general boost in energy. Something that we definitely don't want before bed is extra energy. Not only this but studies have shown people who have high sugar diets will tend to have less deep sleeps than those who don't. Therefore, not too mention all the other health benefits, I recommend you cut down on your sugar intake. This includes not eating any high-sugary foods or drinks too close to bed time. As well as cutting down your sugar throughout the entire day. Ideally you shouldn't be consuming anymore than 90g of sugar each day.

BEDROOM ENVIRONMENT

How we have our bedrooms is a crucial factor in how we're going to sleep. Moreover, what we do in our bedrooms can also have a huge impact on sleep quality. To make it clear I first want to discuss about something called a dawn simulator. It's a device that goes in your bedroom and believe it or not, simulates dawn, or better put; it gradually becomes brighter in the morning to awake you naturally. Then before going to bed it will gradually dim and simulate night fall, which people have believed to increase melatonin in the body and thus sleep better. During studies on dawn simulators it has been found that after a period of time they may slightly increase sleep quality.

Whereas some studies have found that it does almost nothing, in fact people have been known to claim it worsens their quality of sleep. Just to clear this up, the studies that found it to improve sleep quality were small studies and the improvement was miniscule. Therefore it's not worth the risk with a dawn simulator, as they could do more harm than good. As a self experiment I used a dawn simulator for a short while and noticed 0 effects on my sleep.

Now lets dive into the more helpful bedroom tips. First things first, you should only be using your bed/bedroom for sleep. Laying in bed and watching TV or reading a book is a no-no. During these activities your brain will be focussed. Unfortunately this could then lead your mind to associating being in bed with your mind being active and therefore could lead to insomnia. Instead you need to start only using your bedroom for sleep and for sex. Any other activity is prohibited in the bedroom.

Room temperature is our next step. Sleeping whilst too hot is much more difficult than sleeping if you feel cool. This is something that everyone can agree on, sleeping in a hot room can seem like an impossible task even for the best of sleepers. For an insomnia sufferer, it will more than likely be an impossible task. This is why we need to keep our bedrooms cool. This all depends on your geographical location. For me living in England I have almost no worries about ever keeping my bedroom cool. During summer nights I may have my window open but that's about it. A majority of the time in England my bedroom is very cool, seeing as our winter seems to last for 10 months of the year. If you're in a warmer climate though, I would recommend that you invest in a cooling mattress/pad. These work wonders for people living in hot conditions and can make a huge difference in how you sleep. Moreover good ventilation is key so keeping windows open is another good tactic for a cooler bedroom.

Next up we need to talk about noise in the bedroom. How noisey is your room at night? Do you live on a busy road or close to a noisey area? When it comes to noise there's no definitive answer of what works best when it comes to sleep. Some people like the room as quiet as possible, whereas others may want some noise. It's completely dependant on the individual. If you would like noise then I would suggest you go for white noise or pink noise. These are proven to help people sleep and can provide soothing noises making you feel more relaxed. Others may want to go for the television as background noise or in a warmer climate maybe even just the whirring of a fan. Television is to be avoided as we know that watching TV in the bedroom can be an indirect cause of sleep problems. (Once you're completely cured from insomnia, watching TV in bed can become not so much of an issue). For some though they'll sleep better with as little noise as possible. To these people I suggest some softly fitted ear plugs. Ones I use myself are readily available on Amazon and come at a cheap price. Unfortunately you may struggle to sleep with things in your ears so the suggestion then would be to try and block out noise as much as possible from your bedroom.

Finally we have lighting. Just the same with noise, people have different tolerances when it comes to light. Some may want to block out as much light as possible but some can sleep in broad daylight with no issues. To give the best chance I recommend that you block out as much light as possible from your room. This includes upgrading to blackout curtains/blinds. Blocking out the light is going to be majorly beneficial in summer nights when the sun goes down very late and comes up very early. If you're very sensitive to light I would also recommend covering up the cracks around your doors, to stop any light getting in.

BLUE LIGHT

Blue light is essentially the light that is radiated from our mobile phones, televisions, laptops, tablets and so on. As the world seems to grow, our use of blue light technology seems to be growing in direct correlation. Many years ago I myself would barely be on my mobile phone 1 hour per day. As I've aged through the so-called technology era, the use of my mobile phone has dramatically increased. From years ago when using a mobile was just for text messaging, ringing and maybe the odd game. Skip forward to today when it's used for emails, social media, internet, sat-nav, banking, the list goes on and on. Thus meaning that most of us spend too much time staring at our screens all day. Although most people understand that this is a completely unhealthy habit, nobody wants to take steps towards using their phones less.

When it comes to sleep, blue light can be very damaging. Studies have found that blue suppresses the release of melatonin. Melatonin being the hormone released by our bodies to aid with a healthy sleep cycle. It's basically what makes us feel drowsier at night and helps us drift into sleep. In fact all light can be damaging to the amount of melatonin our bodies released. Blue light, though, is found to be much worse than normal light. Essentially the blue light is tricking our brains so that it doesn't understand that it's actually night time.

Next up we need to work on how we can reduce our blue light and when's the best time to put down the phone! In the modern day there's many ways in which we can cut blue light out of our lives. There's apps and filters available on mobile phones that are said to filter out bad blue light. There's also filters available in glasses, for people that use them. I will stress though that the effectiveness of all these is yet to be proven, hence why we should still try and avoid blue light all together. To be on the safe side you should aim to cut down your blue light use throughout the entire day. Not only will this help you getting to sleep but it's a much safer practise and will, more than likely, have a positive impact on your mental health. When it comes to night though I suggest that you avoid looking at blue light for a minimum of 1 hour before you intend on going to bed. Instead take this time to read a book, meditate or take a warm bath. Moreover you should not go on your phone directly after waking up. Avoid your phone for 20 minutes after waking up, to give your body time to acclimatise to natural light.

Always avoid using your phone whilst laid in bed.

BEFORE BED ROUTINE

To cap off the first step, lets run through how you should be preparing yourself to go to bed. Firstly starting with sleep hygiene. Sleep hygiene is something touted by many sleep experts but other experts believe that experiments have proven it useless for chronic insomnia. Instead only helpful towards helping aid normal sleepers into better sleep. Unfortunately if you're at this stage of the book, you're more than likely a bad chronic insomniac and sleep hygiene is going to be pretty much useless at this stage.

Fear not though thanks to Andrew Huberman, a neurobiologist, we have something that definitely can help us drift off. Again, as far as I'm aware, the evidence of this helping insomnia sufferers is limited. However, the elements used in this sleep cocktail, definitely possess the capabilities to reduce anxiety and over-thinking, on top of acting as a mild sedative. Therefore it doesn't take a scientist (maybe it did), to realise this cocktail can be useful for curing chronic insomnia. As a disclaimer, although I am now at a very good stage in my life in terms of sleep. I sleep very well most nights and seem to be able to sleep in different environments with ease. Due to this I have made way with a majority of these lifestyle steps as I am no capable of leading a healthy sleeping pattern without them. This sleep cocktail though is something I have continued to use and will do, possibly for the rest of my life. I tend to use it if I've had a stressful day at work and believe I may be overthinking or just if I want a deep nights sleep. I do not use it every night though and don't recommend anyone to take these supplements, id you don't feel they're needed. The 3 supplements work for me pretty much every time, although I would say it's not a guarantee fix, it's a gigantic help. During my worst insomnia days though it did fail me, hence why this is not the be all and end all cure to insomnia. The cocktail consists of 3 different supplements, all to be taken at the same time, they should be taken roughly 30-60 minutes before you hit the hay. The cocktail consists of the following; Magnesium Threonate, Theanine and Apigenin. All of which have good qualities for helping someone drift off to sleep. Between them they help reduce the chance of sleep anxiety. Sleep anxiety or anxiety of any kind is definitely a top culprit for causing chronic insomnia. When we're in bed and our mind is over-thinking that's the point our insomnia will kick in and sleepless nights will occur. Moreover this cocktail is said not to be habit forming. Meaning that you can use the cocktail without becoming dependant on it and you can come on and off the cocktail as you wish. It's suggested that if you already suffer with extreme dreams or other night-terror type sleep illnesses, don't take these supplements. It can give you pretty wild dreams, take with caution. As always consult a doctor before taking any of these supplements.

LIFESTYLE: SUMMARY

Changing your lifestyle is not going to completely cure your chronic insomnia, not likely anyway. Instead what it will do, through many changes to how you live your life, it will give the following steps a stronger chance of being effective.

Just basic steps such as more exercise and less caffeine can be the difference in getting regular good sleep or regular bad sleep.

SLEEP IMPROVEMENT METHODS

The 2nd stage of our 3 step plan is to use 2 different sleep improvement methods, combined together they can cure almost any insomnia, if given time. These methods are tested and proven to work, they're regularly used by sleep specialists, as a foundation for treating patients.

The 2 separate methods are known as 'sleep restriction' and 'sleep distraction'. Two methods that are said to be the cure for over 90% of insomnia cases. Touted by top-end specialists and both with years of proven results.

SLEEP RESTRICTION

Sleep restriction was invented by Arthur Spielman a psychology professor. Essentially, if you went to a CBT session the first thing they would run through would be the idea of sleep restriction. For the best part, if you're suffering with insomnia, you will more than likely be able to function on less sleep than the average person. Although, people have engrained into their brains from a young age that you need to get 7-8 hours of sleep a night or you'll get fat, have a heart attack, lose brain cells and plenty of other ridiculous statements. People are different and a good percentage of people work at their most optimal on less than 7 hours per night. For example; I know from the months and months of studying my own sleep, I feel at my best rested after 6 – 6.5 hours of sleep.

Anymore and I can feel lethargic, any less and I feel tired. However if I can get a minimum of 5 hours sleep I feel relatively fine the following day. What sleep restriction aims to do is to only have you in your bed for the amount of time you sleep. With insomnia sufferers you'll often find that your hours of sleeping will vary drastically. Your worst nights being no sleep at all, whereas your best nights could be 8 or 9 hours of solid sleep. This is an emphatically poor sleeping pattern, which is going to leave us fighting a losing battle.

How does sleep restriction work then? Well to begin with you'll need your sleep diary at hand. Then using some of your maths skills, work out the average hours you have slept, per night, over the last 2 weeks. Once we have our average figured out, we can work with this average to determine time spent in bed. For example if your average over the last 2 weeks is 6 hours of sleep each night, I want you to start going to bed 6 hours before your alarm. Meaning if you get up at 7am, 1am will be your new bedtime. Understandably at first you may take 30 minutes or so to sleep and this can make you sleep deprived. You'll also have sleepless nights making the following even more difficult to stay awake until your new bed time. Unfortunately this is how it will have to be at first. You'll have to fight through and gradually force your body into this new sleeping pattern. Hopefully getting to a stage in which you fall asleep within a few minutes of your head hitting the pillow. This should stop the overthinking, as you generally become flustered for laying in bed too long, without managing to get to sleep. There are a few rules that need to be followed for sleep restriction. Firstly, you should not allow yourself any less than 5.5 hours of sleep. If you work out your average sleep and it falls under 5.5, then use

5.5 hours as a baseline. The next rule depends on the effectiveness of sleep restriction and how long you've been using this method. It's said that gradually you should allow an extra 15 minutes onto your sleep window. This shouldn't be implemented until you feel 100% comfortable with your sleeping. Once you have reached a stage of consistently falling asleep quickly, you may add 15 minutes on. Again, once you become consistent at this stage you may add another 15 minutes on. However, adding any time on is completely optional. As we already know we all have different levels of optimal sleep. Therefore if you begin a 6.5 hour sleep window and 6.5 hours of sleep is optimal for you, no need to add time on once you become consistent.

Sleep restriction is incredibly effective at curing insomnia. If you pay good money for a sleep clinic or therapist, this will be one of the main methods that they will want to implement with you. You will need to patient though. Although highly effective it's certainly not deemed a quick fix like taking a pain killer for a headache. Instead you'll have to be patient and consistent, it can take many weeks to work but stick with it and you will reap the rewards of better nights sleep.

SLEEP DISTRACTION

As I've just mentioned, sleep restriction is an incredibly popular method used by sleep specialists on insomnia patients. Another method that is arguably just as popular is the sleep distraction method. In terms of my own long, dreadful journey with insomnia, the sleep restriction and distraction methods were by far the most effective. I feel that all the other small lifestyle changes, even including the focus on mentality are just tiny steps towards better sleep, whereas these 2 methods are giant leaps. When combining them all together it becomes a perfect concoction .

What is sleep distraction then? Sleep distraction is the method of trying to distract your brain elsewhere at night, to take away thoughts of sleep anxiety. It's nothing to do with before you go to bed but more when you're actually trying to sleep. This is another method all sleep specialists and clinics will go through with insomnia patients. They will tell you that once in bed you should be falling asleep within 20 minutes. If you realise that you've been laid in bed for 20 minutes or more and you're still awake, get out of bed and leave the bedroom. The intention of this is to break your sleep anxiety, getting you out of bed should stop the thought process of 'I now need to sleep'. Instead, leave the room and go read a book in a separate room for 20 minutes or so. Timings don't need to be exact either, as we don't want to be looking at our phones or to blue light late at night. Once you feel like it could be 20 minutes have a 'quick' glance at your phone or clock. When you leave the bedroom you should do an activity that occupies your mind. The best sleep distraction method is to read a book. A book is a great way to have your mind wander, whilst also not exposing yourself to blue light. Professionals sometimes may also suggest meditation. I would recommend against this personally. Through self-experimentation I found meditation as a sleep distraction method to be impossible. Meditation is an attempt to focus on breathing and allow your stress to drift away. However, by this point you may find that your mind just will not be able to focus on your breathe and thus the sleep anxiety can worsen. Another way to take your mind away could be television. It's blue light so ideally should be avoided but some are less prone to blue light effecting them than others. It can also be the best way to distract yourself. Reading a book would be preferable but you could try both and work with what best suits you.

For this method you must make sure that you leave the bedroom completely. It's not a case of sit on the bedroom floor and read for 20 minutes. Get out of the room all together and go sit or lay down somewhere else. You need to break that mentality of 'I'm in bed I need to be asleep'. Going into a separate room is ideal, as it will help stop thinking in this pattern. Ideally it should completely take your mind away from the fact you should be sleeping at this time, thus reducing your sleep anxiety. You should also repeat this method over and over again through the night. Each time going back to your bed for 20 minutes or so and if you don't feel like you'll sleep, get out the bedroom and repeat the process. You also do not need to be too strict on your overall timings. I've already cleared up that you shouldn't be looking at your phone too often close to bed time. Instead judge it off feeling. If you feel you have been in bed for longer than 20 minutes have a quick glance at your mobile. If it has been longer than 20 minutes you should get out of bed and leave the room. The same applies for the other step, once you've left the room. Once you leave the room you do not need to be on a strict time limit, before you get back into bed. The last thing you need is extra stress of timings etc. Again you should go by how you feel. If you've left the bedroom and read a book, laid on the sofa for 20 minutes but don't feel like you're ready yet to go to bed, simply take a little bit longer. Take as long as you feel you need, until you reach a stage in which you feel tired enough to drift off. As I've previously mentioned you should also repeat this procedure until you manage to get to sleep. The reason I repeat this is that lots of people will tend to give up on sleep distraction if it doesn't work the 1st or 2nd time of asking. Moreover, you may be worried as your wake up gets closer, that leaving your bed is a bad idea. You need to realise if you struggle with insomnia and have laid in bed for over 20 minutes, not managing to fall asleep, you need to break that mental cycle. Although you may think 'It's 2am I need sleep I can't go in to the living room and read at this time'. That's a completely normal and rational way of thinking. However, it will help and it's going to give you a considerable better chance of sleeping, rather than staying in bed and trying to force it.

SLEEP DISTRACTION: SUMMARY

For the record, this is an extremely effective method. Still till this day I follow sleep distraction and can't imagine for some time that I will be giving up on it. Although my sleep is almost always fine now if I do have an off-night, with the sleep distraction I never don't manage to get any sleep whatsoever. Which is why I would always say you need to stick with this method.

SLEEP RESTRICTION: SUMMARY

Sleep restriction is tough to begin with and will take some time of getting used to. It's hugely popular with sleep specialists and arguably the most effective way to treat insomnia. Stick with it for some weeks and I'm confident you'll see huge benefits.

MENTALITY

The 3rd and final stage of our 3 step plan. This is arguably the toughest stage to conquer as mentally no 2 people will ever be the same. Not only this but unfortunately with many mental issues that people suffer from, there's no definitive cure. Millions will suffer from mental illnesses worldwide and although they may get better with therapy, the mental illness will live with them forever. When it comes to cognitive behavioural therapy, which is the therapy that insomniacs will be placed through. They will more than likely run through every single step that I have been through so far, before reverting to looking at your thought processes. This will obviously depend on the severity of your insomnia, what you have already tried and a range of other personal situations. As for me, when I first had CBT, I had already tried so much that my therapist forwarded me on to her supervisor, who then became my therapist.

She basically said everything she wanted to try with me I had already run through and she thought I required more help from her supervisor. However, she also reiterated that I should keep consistent with the practises I had implemented, as they would more than likely benefit me over time. Especially with methods such as sleep restriction it can be weeks and weeks until it begins to take the desired effect.

In terms of how we try and change your thought process most therapists will take a similar approach. As with any type of therapy the first session they will want to know every given detail of your insomnia. How often it occurs, how severe, if you believe anything may have triggered the insomnia and everything else you could think of. The main question I've already mentioned is they'll want to know exactly what you have already tried to battle the insomnia. If you've gotten this far into book or if you have taken to CBT yourself, chances are you've tried almost everything there is to try. Once you run through that with your therapist they'll then try and work out a plan on what the best course is for you to take.

Firstly, if you know or you firmly believe that there was a significant trigger for your insomnia, then help must be tailored towards this. Unfortunately the trigger has already occurred and the insomnia has begun, which means we can't turn back time and stop the trigger from happening. What we can do is tailor your treatment gauged on whatever your specific trigger was. First things first if you know what triggered your insomnia, we need to put a stop to it from triggering you further. If you believe it was from taking recreational drugs then the obvious step would be not to take recreational drugs ever again. If you think working shift patterns have created your insomnia then you'll not be able to work shifts in the future. Unfortunately this can be difficult as some people may be in a career in which they're designed to work shift patterns, which includes working long nights. Not everybody has the capability to work these shift patterns efficiently. For many they'll never be able to work shift patterns and lead a healthy sleeping routine. Hence why if working shift patterns or working nights has triggered your insomnia, your best chance of help would be moving into a career that allows you to sleep the same time everyday. It's a huge step changing jobs and it is possible to cure insomnia, even whilst working shifts but it's much more difficult. Anything else that could possibly have triggered your insomnia will have to be worked on and stopped. Some people claim that work stress's may trigger their sleep problems. Again this could possibly lead to a change in job role or seeing a therapist about work place anxiety. Other triggers could be something such as a catastrophic event happening in your life such as a death of a family member, divorce or anything else that could cause huge mental damage. Again the best cause of action in any of these cases is to seek out therapy. In these cases it may not significantly need to be CBT therapy but instead just a therapist to help treat anxiety and depression. To sum it all up, if you have a specific trigger to your insomnia you need to stop doing whatever it is that's triggered it. If it was from drug taking, stoping taking drugs. If it's from shift patterns, stop working them shift patterns. Once you manage to stop this you can then proceed effectively with the rest of the plan.

For lots of people though they more than likely won't know of a trigger to have bought on the insomnia. This could be due to their never being a trigger or it could just be you're unaware of the trigger ever taking place. Fear not though many people are in the same boat with this one and indeed I was one of the people who was confident that there was no significant trigger, bringing on my insomnia. Our next step in this case is then to try and figure out exactly why our insomnia is occurring. Similar to a trigger but this could be something that is more constant. As I've mentioned previously this is a stage that specifically benefits better from more personalised help. Although I firmly believe in the 3 step process of this book and it will be essentially run through similar methods to a CBT, there's no substitute to seeing a sleep specialist. A sleep specialist will be able to interact with you at this stage, in which they will then be able to gauge what they believe is the root to your insomnia. For the purpose of this book though we'll have to achieve that by going through different processes. Some may be lucky and aware enough as to why they aren't sleeping. Work and general life stress's can often be a culprit. Hopefully if you're confident you know what's causing this stress, you can direct work towards that. For any type of stress, meditation is always a viable option and done properly will help significantly. More about meditation further down in this section. Other ways to help with day-to-day stress's is to speak out. Just talking to a friend or loved one can have a huge impact on how you may look at stress. Remember that often we stress over stuff in our own minds due to built up over-thinking and anxiety. Making a small problem in our minds turn into something we believe as disastrous. Speaking out to someone can help you realise how much you have blown up problems in your head. Moreover, just pouring out your problems to others will help take some weight off your shoulders. If you don't have someone to talk to or aren't comfortable talking to people you know, ring a helpline. Depending on which country you reside there are different helplines and free help services of people that are their just to hear you out.

Moving on then, what if we don't have a clue what is causing our insomnia? This is possibly the worst case scenario, as it's a struggle to battle against something when you have no idea where it's coming from. I mean if you have tried every single step to no avail, with no significant trigger or life stresses causing insomnia, could it mean all help is lost? Well, no it certainly doesn't. We do have a technique which can assist us in finding out exactly what's the route cause of insomnia. This technique involves collecting a reasonably in-depth journal of your day-to-day life. This can work in with your sleep diary, as a much more in-depth version. Everyday you'll need to write down a summary of your entire day. This includes how many hours sleep you got, what time you went to bed, what time you got to sleep, what time you got up, how often you woke during the night and roughly what times. What was on your mind as you fell asleep (if you can remember). If you don't sleep, write down what thoughts went through your head throughout the night.

Please don't write any of this down during the night, as it's time to switch off, just write it down the next morning to the best of your memory.

You also need to jot down throughout your entire day. This can sound like a chore but you can make it much easier and simpler than it has to be. Firstly right down your wake up in the morning. What emotions you had waking up, what you ate for breakfast, how well-rested you feel, if you had any unusual thoughts that normally don't occur. Anything else that made it not feel like your average morning. After this you can then right again at lunch time. Write what happened between breakfast and lunch. Any unusual thoughts, emotions or stress's. Anything significantly different happen at work, how well-rested you feel, what have you had to eat and drink. Repeat this process again after work and then in the evenings. Overall you should be covering your entire day. This doesn't have to be a complete in-depth article every time you right in your journal, it can look like the following.

Time: 8:00am – 12:00pm

Diet

Black coffee
Bowl of cereal

Emotions

Felt slightly down, not usual self.

Other

Feeling tired after bad nights sleep.
Busier at work than normal, causing stress.

This is a very basic journal but it still takes down all the key factors that you'll need to look back on. After 4-6 weeks of this journal, depending on how many bad nights sleep you have will dictate the length of the journal. You can run back on the dates you have noted down as having 0 hours sleep and try spot any patterns.   For example you could notice that everyday you have a busy afternoon at work you don't sleep. This could be due to your mind being too active too late in the day. It could be that every time you wake up feeling down you end up not sleeping that very night. More often than not there will be some sort of pattern correlating between your nights of insomnia. In certain circumstances it could even be something that happened the day before. Moreover it could be something that's happening the following day that's causing the issues. For example you could be aware that the next day you have a busy day at work and it keeps you awake, this could often become a regular pattern. This will generally take 4-6 weeks as mentioned but if you're still struggling seeing a pattern, I would recommend trying for up to 10 weeks. Hopefully we can to the source of your sleep problems and then it becomes much easier to fix.

Unfortunately if you're finding it impossible to still figure out what's causing your insomnia, it will then become very tricky. You almost have 2 options at this point. Well 3 options because in all honesty if you implement both step 1 and 2 correctly, over time that should fix almost any insomnia. The other 2 options are to either go see a specialised sleep doctor/clinic. Again there is no substitute for these specialists, who have worked years in this field and if anyone can get to the bottom of your insomnia, it's a sleep clinic. The other option, is that you can just put your insomnia down to sleep anxiety. Sleep anxiety is the cause of insomnia, we know this, however normally sleep anxiety is bought on by different issues in our lives. What if there's no external issues though and our minds are completely sound? Our only anxiety occurs at night, which is the worry of if we will sleep or not. If this is the case then it's very difficult to get on top of. Again I would recommend either a sleep clinic, therapist or if not I would recommend talking to a friend. The issue with anxiety is that it's very difficult to fix without the aid of someone else. There's books, podcasts and other various ways in which people say they can improve your mental health on your own. I've tried many of these and find them relatively useless. You need someone who you can pour out your anxiety to, someone who will listen and feed you back rational thoughts. Without have any external factors causing your sleep anxiety or no sign of what's causing your insomnia, speaking to a therapist is the way forward. Fortunately, as I have mentioned, if done correctly and for long enough, the first 2 steps should cure almost any insomnia.

There's one more technique though can help you achieve a healthier frame of mind. Besides the way of medication, which many believe is the way forward for anxiety. Especially with new studies evolving claiming things such as psilocybin and MDMA can be incredibly effective for things such as depression and anxiety. However, ideally we want to avoid all such medications and treatments, as understandably these could easily become habit forming for sleep. The only technique left for us to use would be meditation.

MEDITATION

Mediation has increased in popularity drastically over recent years. As more focus is put into our physical and mental health, people are starting to understand the benefits of regular meditation much more. Especially popular with celebrities and entrepreneurs who have hectic lifestyles, meditation is said to be an escape route to inner peace. Meditation can also be beneficial with our sleep anxiety. The process of meditating can help us push away the thoughts of 'I won't sleep tonight' and thus give us a much better chance of a good night's kip. As mentioned previously in the book here is a direct quote from the sleep foundation, about the benefits of meditation and sleep.

Research suggests that various types of meditation can help improve insomnia, and may even improve sleep quality for those without existing sleep problems. Mindfulness meditation, in particular, appears to improve sleep quality and reduce daytime disturbance in people with chronic insomnia and older adults. In the long term, these improvements may be comparable to effects seen from sleep medication or other established methods

for insomnia treatment. Like other sleep treatments, a main goal of meditation is to take the pressure off to fall asleep.

Meditation is also a technique that is practised by therapists for many different types of mental issues. Specifically being used to help people with depression and anxiety. Although some may believe that their insomnia is nothing to do with their mental well-being, it's more than likely that subconsciously this isn't the case. Without realising you can suffer from hidden depression and mental health illnesses, that will in turn increase the chances of insomnia. Which is yet another reason meditation is a valuable tool for anyone struggling with sleep issues. All of this is well and good but it still leaves us with some incredibly important questions we need to run through, in relation to sleep and meditation. How often should I meditate? How long for? When should I meditate? How do you meditate? Plus many more questions I intend to answer in this section.

Firstly we need to discuss how we should meditate. There's actually a tonne of different variations out their nowadays. There's meditation done in hot environments, meditation done in yoga and even meditation retreats. For us though we're just using the most basic form of meditation. One that we can use easily and any time during the day, on our own, irrelevant of environment and equipment. Here's my exact passage from previously in the book that runs through a simple meditation technique.

Let's look at how to meditate, as it's something I'm not very efficient at I imagine this to be somewhat of a learning curve. To being with you're supposed to find somewhere peaceful and quiet, (already sounding difficult in my house hold.) Then you need to get comfortable, either seated or laid down it doesn't matter but you need to be as comfortable as possible. When most people think about meditation they think of a monk sat on a rug with legs crossed and hands raises either side looking like a salt bae hand, well that's not necessarily how it goes. The aim is to be as comfortable as possible, whether that be with legs crossed or straight out. You can be on the floor, a chair or a sofa it doesn't particularly matter. Then you need to set yourself a timer, some kind of alarm that will alert you but in a gentle manner. You don't want to be coming out of a peaceful meditation session with a siren blasting off in your ear. Try get a soothing alarm or something that even just softly vibrates. Set your alarm to however long you plan to meditate, although for beginners it's recommended around 5 minutes. Once you get used to meditating you can increase the time frame. When the clock is set you can begin to meditate.

Start by closing your eyes and focus on your breathing. Breathe slowly in and out, focus on each *breath, think about the breathing, don't worry about the length of breath or if it's through your nose/mouth. Just think about breathing in and then breathing out, nice and slow. Try to focus on your breathing and gradually other things will slip into your mind, don't worry it's supposed to happen. Once you realise you're no longer thinking about your breathing, try get back to it. Push your other thoughts to the side and focus on your breathing in and breathing out. These thoughts will continue occurring but don't worry it's natural. Some thoughts you'll wonder how it even came to your head but allow it to come and then push it aside. Don't beat yourself up if you struggle to concentrate on breathing at all, it's natural, the more you meditate the more efficient you'll become. Once your timer goes off gradually come back. Slowly open your eyes and come back to the world. Don't worry if at first you don't feel much from it, it takes time and practise for meditation to work it's magic.*

It's a very simple and basic process but is the most commonly used meditation method. In this technique I mention that you should be setting your timer for 5 minutes and you can increase this as you become more efficient. This is just a rough guideline, if you feel like straight off the bat you can meditate for longer, then by all means go for it. The only reason I suggest to start with 5 is that it's a much more reasonable time for a beginner. To begin with even 5 minutes can seem like an age so don't beat yourself up if you find yourself wondering how long you have left midway through. Also don't beat yourself up if even after plenty of practise meditating you still feel like 5 minutes is an adequate amount of time. For some, 5 minutes can indeed be enough and for others they may want longer, if you're achieving what you set out to achieve from meditating, then it's all well and good. In fact at first it's going to feel like meditation is relatively pointless. It can take many weeks of meditating before you start to feel any type of benefits. Some will again find it much quicker than others, unfortunately some people tend to overthink much more than others. Stick with it and trust the process, in the long run you'll be glad that you did.

How often should you meditate and what's the best times? There's actually not much focus on what's the best times you should be meditating. Ideally for it to help with sleep I recommend that you meditate late on in the evening. Hopefully relieving some anxiety before it's time to go to bed. This doesn't necessarily mean you have to meditate immediately before bed or within a certain timeframe but ideally late on in the evening. Fear not though if you're unable to meditate in the evenings for whatever reason, you can still achieve great benefits from meditating anytime of day. Meditation is there to help relieve stress and reduce anxiety, whether this be in the morning or night, it can still achieve this. As for how often you should meditate, I recommend for the most effective method that you meditate twice a day, everyday. Ideally these times should in the evening as previously mentioned, the other time can be any point throughout the day. However meditating twice a day, at any point, will have significant mental benefits.

There's other types of meditation out there, not just the most basic types. People will meditate during yoga and yoga poses, which is an increasingly popular type to meditate. Yoga is focussed around breathing anyway so it slots well into meditation and is said to increase the ability both in yoga and meditation. The only negative with yoga and meditation is that I recommend you need to do this in a class. Simply trying to learn yoga and meditation on your own can be a difficult task.

Another type of helpful meditation can be visualisation meditation. This is a personal favourite of mine and one that can be a brilliant way to battle against insomnia. As with basic meditation I recommend that you begin by setting a timer at around 5 minutes. Although visualisation meditation can be a little more tricky, I still believe 5 minutes is a good target to aim for, to begin with. With this type of meditation the aim is to think of a peaceful place, whilst using your other senses to visualise it even better.

Try think of a calm beach, imagine that you're hearing the waves, breathe in and feel the salty, sea air, try to feel the sun on your skin. As I said this is much more difficult, especially at an evening, as your mind may be fully fixated on the thought of sleep. However it can be much more powerful. If you are able to completely transport your mind to somewhere else then, you'll be able to battle insomnia much more effectively.

The next type of meditation I want to discuss is the progressive relaxation meditation. This is similar to what we discussed previously in the book, involving the relaxation of muscles in our body. A method that can commonly be taught in the military services as a way to help sleep in tough situations. For this method you need to start by again closing your eyes and firstly steady your breathing. Then either working your way from the bottom to the top or vice-versa, start by relaxing all of your bodies muscles. Tense one muscle group, for example your arm, then release the tension. Repeat a few times so that you arm feels fully relaxed and softens. You need to complete this method from your feet all the way up to your face, gradually releasing tension throughout the entire body. Hence the name, progressive relaxation therapy. The full aim of this method is to release tension out of the body and leave you completely in a state of calm. It's a way to relieve stress and tension, often being used to unwind before bed time. Which makes it a great technique for insomniacs.

Finally we have focussed meditation. This is our final meditation process for helping sleep but there are multiple other meditation methods out there. I would always encourage people to try as many as possible, some will work better for others. This method entails concentrating on one of your senses. For example you could go with your hearing. Play some soothing sounds or something significant like a gong being hit, then make sure your full focus is on listening to the sounds. Another good example could be using your sight to focus on something. Possibly a calm candle burning, just stare at the candle focus on it flowing forwards and backwards. This method can be very difficult to focus and for beginners you'll often find your mind wanting to wander. Again, as with starting out on any type of meditation, you should try and just hit a few minutes at first. Don't beat yourself up if it feels difficult and ineffective, over time you will become much more efficient for sure.

That's all the types of meditation that I would recommend for people suffering with insomnia. There are still plenty of other different techniques out there but these are the top ones for helping with sleep. Ideally you should be trying to meditate twice a day, making sure that one of them slots is late in the evening. This way it will help you unwind before heading to bed. Although if for some reason that's not plausible then you can meditate any time throughout the day and still feel significant benefits. As for timings I always say to start off just aiming for 5 minutes of meditation each time. If you can do more then great, if you struggle to do the full 5 minutes it's understandable. You will become more efficient over time. Meditation is definitely one of the most powerful tools you can use for achieving better mental health and being rid of any anxiety or depression. However, as I will reiterate for deep problems with anxiety or any mental health issues such as insomnia, personalised therapy will always be the most effective. No book or set structure can replace a human being who is able to communicate back to you and help personalise your treatment.

RELEASING ANXIETY

This is my final tip for dealing with anxiety based around sleep and insomnia. It's a method very well-known and very common but it works very well. Something that I have used many times in my life and if I come into hard times today, wouldn't hesitate to use. It's based around of releasing your anxiety, through writing down emotions and stress's. A technique that can be adapted by different people, however, the general method will always be the same. Here is the exact technique that I will always use.

Begin by writing down, in short bullet points, all of the worries that are in your head. The list can be as long as you want or just very short, no worry is too big or too small. For example you could write you want a new car, you want a new job, you want to lose weight. All are reasonable worries, that are found to be very common. As I said no issue is too small or too big to write down. Once you have all of the problems written down, go down the list and cross out all of the problems that are out of your control. In other words things that can't be helped. Then out of the issues that you have left on your list, circle the one that bothers you the most. For example it could be the fact that you feel overweight. Circle that issue and then using another piece of paper or different page on your phone, write down how you can combat this issue. For example if you want to lose weight, you would write stuff such as go on a diet, go to the gym, start running 3 times a week etc. Once you write down how to combat this issue, you then need to implement everything that you have just written down. This way you should start notice a difference and you'll now have a clear path to end your main concern in life. Just starting on the path will give you a significant mental boost. Hopefully you end up at a stage in which you completely fix the issue in hand. At this point I want you to re-write the list and start the process again.

OVERVIEW

That's the full 3 step plan covered and I'm extremely confident in it's ability to cure almost any insomnia. All 3 steps are of a high importance and they will all work well with each other, to give you the best result. Although, just 1 of these steps could have the ability to completely cure you, depending on the severity of your insomnia. In fact, sleep restriction and sleep distraction used together are said to be the most effective way to treat almost all insomnia.

The first step of our course is to change your lifestyle. The reason we begin with this is that our way of living can have a significant relationship on how well we're sleeping. If we aren't living following the correct procedures and habits, then we are already destroying our chances of a healthy sleeping pattern. Changing our lifestyle may seem like a chore and something that could take a whole lot of work. However all I ask is that you make many subtle changes to your daily routine. All of these small, subtle changes combined can dramatically increase your chance of the next steps having a positive effect. Things such as decreasing your caffeine intake and ingesting certain supplements can often be an easy fix for insomniacs. With this first step, you can quite easily implement all of the lifestyle changes at once. Although if you'd prefer, you can gradually make one change at a time. Once bringing in the changes I want you to continually work with them until they become a natural habit. In other words they're just part of your everyday lifestyle and you no longer need to actually think about them, instead you just do it. This can take weeks to achieve so patience is important for our first step.

The next step is our sleep improvement methods. These can quite easily be implemented along with step 1 concurrently. The 2 methods that we concentrate on are the sleep distraction and sleep restriction techniques. Both extremely popular methods used by top sleep experts, across the globe. Both of them also have a history of brilliant results, with insomnia patients. Therefore making them the foundation of this 3 step course. Quite simply put sleep distraction is a method in which you only allow yourself 20 minute slots in bed, to try for sleep. If after 20 minutes you're still awake get up and leave the room for 20 minutes. When you leave the room you should try and distract your mind, with something like reading a book. Repeat this process over and over. The reason for this method is that laying in bed longer than 20 minutes is when you will begin to get flustered and your mind will race. Also it's believed if you aren't asleep within 20 minutes then you simply aren't yet ready to go to sleep. Sleep restriction is also a method that is pretty self explanatory. The aim of sleep restriction is to restrict the amount of time you're spending in bed. Sleep restriction works of the thesis that you should only ever be in bed when you're asleep. Therefore if you restrict the amount of time you spend in bed, you will restrict the amount of time you're in bed awake. Hopefully by now you can see the easy relation that sleep distraction and sleep restriction both have. They both intend to only have you in bed asleep and not in bed forcing yourself to sleep. With sleep restriction to begin with you should use your sleep diary, to work out an average time you actually sleep. This can be an average over 2 to 6 weeks or anything in between these margins. Once you have your average, you then need to make sure that you're only in bed for that set amount of time. For example if you average 6 hours of sleep, go to bed 6 hours before your alarm. This takes some time as at first it'll take you time to get to sleep and you may end up feeling exhausted. After some time though, you should eventually be falling asleep almost as soon as your head hits the pillow. Once you reach a stage of comfortably sleeping the 6 hours you're in bed, taking minimal amount of time to fall asleep, you can begin increasing your time in bed. This should start by increasing your time in bed in 15 minute increments.

Gradually increase the amount of time you spend in bed, until you reach what you believe to be your optimal amount of sleep. Essentially stop as soon as you feel well rested, almost every day. If you don't feel like you need to increase the time you spend in bed, then you don't have to increase. Work within your own optimal timing. I can't stress enough the importance of both these techniques and how much they will help if followed over time.

The third and final step is to try and help your mental thoughts and processes. This is arguably the most difficult step of them all, as our minds will all work in completely different ways to one another. Although extremely difficult it's not impossible to help ourselves when it comes to how we think. Sleep anxiety is what causes chronic insomnia, in a majority of cases. Our aim in this step is to figure out what's triggering our sleep anxiety. That's why at first we work on finding your insomnia trigger. For some lucky people they'll already be aware of the trigger and therefore can just put a stop to it easily. For example if you believe your insomnia was bought on by excessive alcohol consumption, then stop drinking alcohol. For others though , a trigger may be completely unknown and therefore we want to try and figure out what the trigger is. This is why I run through a helpful journal. You need to jot down thought processes, working habits and diet, along with anything else they may be significant on any given day. Hopefully this way we can notice a pattern as to what is happening on the days you cannot sleep. After you know your trigger or even if you can't figure out one, you'll move onto the next stage, which is reducing overall anxiety and depression. To do this I do suggest firstly that you see a therapist, hopefully depending on which country you reside, you may be able to get this for free. If not then you can talk to a friend and you'd be surprised how much offloading to someone regularly can help. Furthermore you can even write down your emotions on a regular basis. Writing down your feelings, gives you an insight of what's really bugging you and you can use this to try figure out solutions. Moreover writing down your feelings may open your eyes to how trivial your problems actually are. Finally for this step I run through meditation. Meditation is becoming ever more popular across the planet. This is due to it's significant benefits it has on our mental health. On top of this, research has found that meditation can be very effective at helping us sleep. Therefore I suggest that you meditate twice a day. Preferably one of these meditation sessions should occur later on in the evening. Doing so will help relieve stress and anxiety, allowing us to drift off much more peacefully.

PATIENCE

With this 3 step plan there's one element that needs to be reiterated for you to achieve the best results. When it comes to insomnia and sleep issues, the fact is that it will more than likely have a very damaging effect on your life. It can make working a struggle, have you missing social activities and completely destroy your mental health. Therefore when it comes to fixing insomnia most people want the fix to come as quickly as possible. With plenty even expecting the fix to come within a matter of a few weeks.

As you've probably already come to realise, sorting out your insomnia is not going to be a quick fix. It requires experimentation of multiple different methods, over different timescales. It always requires a significant amount of patience. For some people they may be rid of their insomnia within a few weeks but for most it will take months and months. This is irrelevant of whether you choose my plan, another plan or straight for CBT. To go from a chronic insomniac to a regular sleeper it's going to take a long time. That's why I ask anyone following this 3 step course that you be patient with it and allow enough time for it to work, before dismissing it.

AFTER CARE

Once completing the 3 step program I sincerely hope that you have achieved what you set out for. That being that you have a a healthy sleeping pattern and your life is no longer significantly affected by insomnia. Unfortunately this is no 100% guarantee and there may be a few people out there who will always struggle somewhat with insomnia.

Hopefully for these people if this book doesn't completely cure your sleep woes, it will, as a minimum, help lessen them. After you have completed all 3 steps of this course and you feel like you're finally over your insomnia, you'll want to start gradually getting back to a normal life. By normal life I mean you want to slowly get rid of some control measures, that you have implemented to help better sleep. Instead we want to become as close to a naturally, healthy sleeper as possible. We don't want to be constantly worried about going to bed the exact same time 365 days a year. Moreover we want to allow ourselves to be able to do things like watch television in bed. Hence why it's important, once you're in a good place, to do things correctly and make sure that you can slowly achieve this goal but without slipping back into a bad place.

For this part of the book, again I'm wanting to take it step by step and run through each section so that you understand the full concept of our aftercare section. The worst thing that could possibly happen during this is that you slip back into a bad insomnia cycle. This doesn't mean that you start having the odd night of bad sleep. The odd night of bad sleep is perfectly normal and providing it is just the odd night, won't cause any damage to our healthy sleeping pattern. However if you slip into a stage in which you're having regular nights of very little sleep or even just some nights with 0 sleep, we need to go back full throttle on our 3 step program.

To begin with is our lifestyle. I've already gone through in the overview that ideally your lifestyle steps should eventually become 2nd nature to you. This means that you shouldn't be thinking about them, you should just be doing them naturally. All of the lifestyle steps, I believe are also relatively easy to continue for the rest of your life. However there may be times when we want to break the rules, as it fits in with our schedule. Firstly we spoke about caffeine intake. For this plan I suggest that if possible you take your caffeine down to 0. However most people like a caffeine boost in the mornings, therefore you can have some caffeine but restrict it to just mornings. You shouldn't be having any caffeine within 10 hours of your bedtime, which in my eyes is a step that can easily be continued forever. However if you feel that you do need a boost of energy later in the afternoon than usual, by all means you can. Just make sure that this isn't a regular occurrence, make sure it's not too close to bed time and make sure it's not too much caffeine. This can also be done if you're comfortable with caffeine and you're at a stage in which you feel like a healthy sleeper. If you take caffeine later than usual and you have a bad nights sleep, then you should go back to the original of having caffeine only in early mornings. This same methodology goes for all types of dietary changes you have made. This includes eating sugar close to bed time andeating larger meals closer to bed time. As you become more comfortable in your sleep you can start to alleviate some of these steps, hopefully not damaging your sleeping pattern.

One more step that you can tinker with is your bedroom environment itself. In terms of noise, darkness and heat of the bedroom, I would suggest you keep that the same. As for bedroom activities though, this is another step in which you can, if you wish, gradually alleviate. Now I definitely don't suggest you all of a sudden use your bed as your work office or stay in bed consistently through the day. I do suggest that you start to be a little easier on certain rules.   Certain activities such as watching TV and reading a book can gradually be introduced to the bedroom environment. It's common practice for most people to have televisions in their bedrooms nowadays so to ban yourself from watching TV in bed for life seems somewhat unrealistic. I still recommend that you try and keep the exposure down, as much as possible. This is something that I gradually introduced myself and during my own aftercare program, television was the first step I eased. Gradually allowing a little more time watching TV in bed each. Firstly starting with just 30 minutes per week, then 1 hour and increasing it as I saw fit. This obviously wasn't a set time, as some weeks I may not want to watch television in bed at all. These are the times that I capped so I suggest that you do the same. Again as with every step if you feel it starts sending you back into bad sleeping habits, reverse the changes.

The final lifestyle change that I recommend you can alleviate would be the sleep cocktail. All 3 supplements which taken together are a brilliant way of helping ease you off to sleep as recommended by Andrew Huberman. It's believed that this cocktail is non habit forming. Something that I can vouch for as I've taken these supplements, coming on and off them, without having any difficulties sleeping without. Therefore I am confident that as you become a better sleeper, you can rid of these supplements, without suffering any negative effects. I still recommend, though, that you keep these supplements at the ready. It's a way of easing your mind, knowing that if you do slip into a bad night taking these pills will be a big aid to a better nights sleep.

These are all the lifestyle changes that I recommend you to ease off. By all means if you don't feel the need to ease any of them off, you can continue using all these steps for as long as you see fit. The other steps that we mentioned, such as lowering your blue light exposure and exercising more often, I would suggest that you keep these in place. These aren't just useful ways of helping you sleep better but they'll also benefit your general health. Exercising regularly is a fantastic way to keep yourself in good shape and keep your bodyweight down. Whilst also doing wonders for your mental health. Whereas having less blue light exposure is going to be better on your eyes and again will have a positive effect on your mental health. Both of these are great steps to follow for life, in my opinion. Although if you want to tinker with either, it shouldn't have a detrimental effect on your sleeping habits.

The next step of the 3 part plan is to implement both the sleep distraction and sleep restriction methods. These are arguably the most important and most effective steps. This is why these are also the most difficult steps to alleviate on our aftercare section of the course. Sleep distraction is a method that, in all honesty, you should keep in place forever. The simple method of leaving your bed within 20 minute slots can be an absolute life saver, when it comes to getting a good nights sleep. It doesn't necessarily mean that you have to be as strict though. As a general rule I like to say when you first get in bed allow yourself more time than you normally would. In fact allow yourself as much time as you see fit when you first get into bed. Then, if you start to feel you're getting anxious about sleeping, begin the sleep distraction method. Still try and stick with the 20 minute slots at this point but you don't have to be overly concerned about exact timing. This is a method that should really be used for life and can work wonders for your sleep. Still months down the line from me first being able to have a healthy sleeping pattern, I still use sleep distraction on my difficult nights. Due to using sleep distraction I no longer ever have nights of 0 hours sleep. Sometimes, rarely, I have difficult nights in which I may only get 4 hours or so but I believe that to be completely normal. Not only normal but very sustainable and has no adverse impact on my life.

Next up was the sleep restriction method, again another self-explanatory technique. Sleep restriction as we have already spoken about will already begin to alleviate itself if you follow the program correctly. It should have you gradually increasing your time in bed by 15 minute increments. This is down to your own personal choice and how much time you feel you need in bed to be at your most optimal. With sleep restriction though it needs to be very specific and detailed timelines to work correctly. However, as we enter our aftercare program we don't want to be so restricted forever. Instead we want to allow ourselves much more leeway. By leeway I mean that you should no longer restrict yourself to say 6 hours in bed or whatever time slot you're used to. Instead use this timing as a basis, try and keep to roughly your optimal sleeping times. However if you feel like you're tired and ready for bed earlier than usual, go to sleep earlier. If you want a later night, then take a later night and if you want a lay in, do it. We want to allow ourselves sleeping methods similar to that of a normal sleeper. Normal sleepers do not restrict themselves and just sleep/go to bed whenever they see fit. We want to achieve the same but whilst still remaining some level of sleep consistency. If you drift too far away from the original method, you may slip back into poor sleeping habits. As a simple summary, try and always stick to your optimal sleeping time but if you feel like you really need to change it up, go for it.

Finally we have the mentality side of the plan, which is the 3rd and final step. Changing your thought processes around sleep and anxiety is the most difficult thing to do. Hopefully the other steps in this plan will make it substantially easier but it can still be extremely difficult. Firstly I mentioned that you need to try and figure out if and what your trigger may be causing insomnia. This is something that changed during your everyday life and doing so has effected your brain, in a way, so that you struggle to sleep. This can be things such as recreational drug taking, alcohol or working shift patterns. If you figure out your trigger, then the cure to your insomnia will become much easier. Simply don't ever trigger your insomnia again, by stopping whatever it is. If it's excessive alcohol then stop drinking too much, if it's working shifts, stop working shifts. It's that simple, this should never change. Other ways in which your mentality could be hurting your sleep pattern would be anxiety or depression. For this the best way to help is mainly to go for a therapist, they will always be the most influential on your mind, as they can personalise a plan and react to your emotions. However, if this isn't feasible for you, I suggest either talking to a friend or jotting down problems that you have in your life. All of these methods for treating anxiety should be sustained even after your insomnia is gone. That is until you feel completely relieved of your anxiety, this can take a very long time. The final part of the whole program is to meditate, which will help alleviate mental stress and anxiety. For our aftercare program meditation needs to be self-managed. You can judge for yourselves how much you need to keep meditating and if you need to continue. For me, I have continued meditating and believe that I will meditate for the rest of my life. The benefits that I found through meditation are something that I find incredibly valuable, in many different aspects of my day to day life. If you believe that it's not providing much benefit at all and making the time can be a hinderance, by all means you can rid of meditation from your schedule. Remember though, meditation will generally become more effective the longer you stick with it so it's important to bare that in mind.

AFTERCARE: SUMMARY

Aftercare is almost as important as the plan itself. The 3 step plan is geared towards completely curing you of any sleep issues you may have. Specifically insomnia. After you are cured though, the next important step is to gradually get to a normal sleeping habit. We do not want to live our entire lives under restrictions and limitations, just to help us sleep. Instead we want to allow ourselves a normal life, in which sleep is something we no longer worry about, it's just something we're naturally good at.

To do this we want to slowly alleviate steps out of our life. The important pointer you need to take from this stage is that you should alleviate gradually. Alleviating multiple steps concurrently is bad practise and will more than likely lead you back into a nasty sleeping habit. Instead you should focus on specifically one step at a time. Once you feel like you no longer need to rely on this change and your sleeping is still healthy, you can begin to ease off other steps. It's a gradual process that can take many months to completely ween you into a normal sleeper. The process is long but it will be worth it.

FINAL THOUGHTS

Insomnia is a terribly cruel illness and one I know too much about. Throughout my years I have suffered with multiple different batches of insomnia, culminating in a terrible stage, which lasted over a year. During this I was suffering from multiple sleepless nights every week and consistently having my life affected by lack of sleep. I decided to take action and research deeper into insomnia, how it works and what's the best way to combat it. I realised there are many steps to take, before seeking help from a medical professional.

All relatively small steps that can help you sleep better, without making drastic changes to your lifestyle. Each step I took, I researched how and why it should work. I also detailed down how I found each method to work on my own insomnia and if I felt they're worth while for other insomniacs. During this period, unfortunately for me, none of the small steps that I took had any positive, long-lasting effect on my insomnia. However, I am well aware that many people can have positive, long-lasting effects, hence why I details these steps in the book.

For me, though, I then began to dig much deeper into insomnia. I sought out professional advice and began to learn more about the ideas of sleep restriction and sleep distraction. I then decided to completely focus on these methods. After delving deeper into them, I soon realised these are the 2 methods that are predominantly used by sleep specialists worldwide. With both of them having plenty of proven results over many years. Next I decided to devise my full plan on how I was going to treat myself from insomnia. This was partly due to my therapist consistently letting me down and being put on big wait lists. Instead I took it into my own hands.

The first step of the plan was to work on all of the things I had used, in the first half of the book. These little steps may not be the full cure for insomnia but they will give the later steps a much better chance of working. Obviously I would only use lifestyle changes that I had seen enough promise in, from self-experimentation. After all these steps were in place I hit the distraction and restriction methods simultaneously. These were my toughest steps to follow, as restricting time in bed to such a short space of time was a killer. Then with sleep distraction I found it difficult to keep dragging myself out of bed, when I couldn't sleep. However I did find that these methods worked very quickly for me. I still didn't feel like I was 100% satisfied or 100% over my insomnia, though. At this point I decided to focus more on the mental aspect of insomnia. This bought to my attention the possibility of triggers. A trigger is simply something significant that bring on insomnia. Something such as recreational drugs or working shift patterns can be a trigger to insomnia. The obvious way to deal with these triggers is to stop whatever it is that is triggering it in the first place. Unfortunately not everyone has a trigger or some may have but not be aware of it. There are ways in which you can help look for a trigger, which is highly recommended, as if you find the trigger beating insomnia becomes a whole lot easier. Apart from triggers, there are other ways in which our minds can cause insomnia. Essentially, anxiety or sleep anxiety is the biggest issue with insomnia. Anxiety can be concerns that we have in our life, that play on our mind, causing us stress and making us feel down. Due to this our minds can be in overdrive at night time. Not allowing us to wind down and drift off into sleep. I quickly learnt that to battle anxiety it's much more difficult without the help of another person. To beat anxiety, purely by yourself, it's always going to be a tough task, instead it's much easier if you get aid from someone else. This is because they can personalise their helps towards individuals, as well as listen to what a person has to say. Hence why I do suggest at this point to try and speak to some sort of therapist but if that's not possible then even talk to a friend. People from an outsiders point of view will see things different to yourself and it can help dramatically. Other ways to rid of anxiety include writing down your emotions or meditation. Both can be very useful and effective, while neither need any outside help. If in fact you don't feel like you have an anxiety or issues but you still can't sleep due to mental issues, this is sleep anxiety. Something that I also suffered with. Sleep anxiety is when you feel fine throughout the day but come night time you will begin to get anxious, about if you're going to sleep or not. Sleep anxiety is difficult to deal with, in fact It's the most difficult issue to deal with, when it comes to insomnia. Again my best advice for this would be to see a therapist. However I managed to defeat sleep anxiety by myself, purely by using the first 2 steps and then following a meditation program. With meditation I would meditate twice a day, both later on in the day. Once after work and once just before bed time. I definitely feel like the meditation was the cherry on the top of the cake when, it come to fixing my insomnia. However it wouldn't have been very helpful without the significant lifestyle changes I had already made.

All this information is how my book has came about. After suffering with insomnia I understand how awful it can be and in all honesty I always felt that certain books or certain 'specialists', don't understand how impactful it is on our lives. Hence why I wanted to write this book from a perspective of someone who completely understands. Not only someone who understands but someone who has been in the deepest, darkest stages of sleep problems but come out the other end. Now my sleeping pattern is completely healthy, I have no restrictions in place. I can watch TV in bed, I can lay in on days off and I need no help with supplements or vitamins. This is all thanks to the plan that I have provided. I can only say that I hope this helps for you reading this book and you stick with the plan long enough to work it's magic.

I thank you for taking the time to read my book and hope you found what you came looking for. As always I recommend you listen to podcasts with Matthew Walker and Dr. Hugh Selsick. If not podcasts, search out for their information online. Both of which are full of knowledge and specialists in sleep. Again, I thank you for reading.

Printed in Great Britain
by Amazon

75667804R00102